Praise for *I Found Love*

"I Am Second's storytelling ability shines throughout *I Found Love*, bringing truth, hope, and strength during times of uncertainty. These stories of redemption, especially the dramatic and miraculous testimony of my friend Ryan Ries, are exactly what we need to hear today."

—Brian "Head" Welch, legendary Korn guitarist

"*I Found Love* is a gripping read and retell of the greatest love story of all time. The variety and scope of the stories included prove there is hope out there for anyone and everyone. We all long to belong and feel loved . . . and the reality is, that is possible with God. I encourage anyone who is hurting or lonely to dive into the honest and true stories included in this book."

—Autumn Miles, author and host of the podcast *The Autumn Miles Show*

"*I Found Love* includes the story of my dear friend and combat veteran Chad Robichaux, who is as tough as they come. But even a battle-hardened American Spartan can be brought to his knees by an invisible enemy. Chad's life is one that realized Jesus Christ had to be the champion, the Warrior of his heart, in order for him to find true strength."

—Lieutenant Colonel Allen B. West (US Army, retired), member 112th US Congress

"I am a curious soul. I want to know a character's history. *I Found Love* takes the stories from I Am Second's website, which we all love, and takes them to a whole other level by adding details and backstory not found in the films. I love that I can consume the book at my own pace. All at once or in bite-sized pieces."

—Tiffini Kilgore, founder, House of Belonging; author, *Misfit Table*

"In *I Found Love* the common thread of all the I Am Second stories is I Found Jesus. When we fall in love with Jesus everything else will fall into place. Only when we stop wanting to be first can God start being first. 'He must increase I must decrease' (John 3:30)."

—Dave Robbins, musician with Blackhawk and the Outlaws

"With diversity of stories and added background information, *I Found Love* appeals to just about anyone. Whether you had love, are in love, or are searching for love, this book provides clarity of just where the purest of love is found."

—Carol Bevil, *Fuel Body Feel Soul* blogger

I FOUND
LOVE

TRUE STORIES OF DISCOVERING LOVE,
BELONGING, AND FRIENDSHIP

Doug Bender

NELSON
BOOKS

An Imprint of Thomas Nelson

Published in Nashville, Tennessee, by Nelson Books, an imprint of Thomas Nelson. Nelson Books and Thomas Nelson are registered trademarks of HarperCollins Christian Publishing, Inc.

Published in association with the literary agency of Wolgemuth & Associates, Inc.

Thomas Nelson titles may be purchased in bulk for educational, business, fund-raising, or sales promotional use. For information, please e-mail SpecialMarkets@ThomasNelson.com.

Any Internet addresses, phone numbers, or company or product information printed in this book are offered as a resource and are not intended in any way to be or to imply an endorsement by Thomas Nelson, nor does Thomas Nelson vouch for the existence, content, or services of these sites, phone numbers, companies, or products beyond the life of this book.

Unless otherwise noted, Scripture quotations are taken from the Holy Bible, New International Version®, NIV®. Copyright © 1973, 1978, 1984, 2011 by Biblica, Inc.™ Used by permission of Zondervan. All rights reserved worldwide. www.zondervan.com. The "NIV" and "New International Version" are trademarks registered in the United States Patent and Trademark Office by Biblica, Inc.™

Scripture quotations marked NIRV are from the New International Reader's Version. Copyright © 1995, 1996, 1998, 2014 by Biblica, Inc.®. Used by permission. All rights reserved worldwide.

Scripture quotations marked ESV are from the ESV® Bible (The Holy Bible, English Standard Version®), copyright © 2001 by Crossway, a publishing ministry of Good News Publishers. Used by permission. All rights reserved.

Scripture quotations marked NLT are from the *Holy Bible*, New Living Translation. © 1996, 2004, 2007, 2013 by Tyndale House Foundation. Used by permission of Tyndale House Publishers, Inc., Carol Stream, Illinois 60188. All rights reserved.

ISBN 978-1-4041-1568-2 (custom)
ISBN 978-1-4002-2136-3 (eBook)
ISBN 978-1-4002-1038-1 (HC)

Library of Congress Cataloging-in-Publication Data

Names: Bender, Doug, author.
Title: I found love : true stories of discovering love, belonging, and friendship / Doug Bender.
Description: Nashville : Nelson Books, 2020. | Includes bibliographical references. | Summary: "I Found Love is the highly anticipated new book from I Am Second, gathering together stories of people who searched everywhere for fulfillment and wholeness and found it only when they surrendered to God"-- Provided by publisher.
Identifiers: LCCN 2020021816 | ISBN 9781400210381 (hc) | ISBN 9781400210398 (ebook)
Subjects: LCSH: Christian biography.
Classification: LCC BR1700.3 .B465 2020 | DDC 277.3/0830922 [B]--dc23
LC record available at https://lccn.loc.gov/2020021816

Printed in the United States of America

21 22 23 24 25   LSC   10 9 8 7 6 5 4 3 2 1

To Norm Miller who read <u>John 12:32</u> and knew
God wanted him to lift up Jesus in his city.
To Nathan Sheets and Adam Leydig who
took Norm's ideas and infused their creative
vision that still inspires us today.
To our many donors whose partnership
enables us to spread the love of Jesus.
To Tom Gabe. We miss you dearly.

Acknowledgments

A special thanks to the entire I Am Second team. Every book is a group project, but this one has a particularly large, creative, and passionate team of people behind it. Thank you for bringing all your many talents to the table.

A big thanks to I Am Second's many fans, donors, and supporters who continue to spread the stories of those who found the love of Jesus.

Also a huge thanks and much love to Catherine. Your endless support means more than I can ever put to words. And thanks to

ACKNOWLEDGMENTS

Bethany, Samuel, Isabella, and Jesse, who gave up time with Dad so he could write a book. I love you all.

And once again, thanks to Nancy Nelson whose knack for fixing my typos, grammar, and spelling is ever so appreciated.

Stanley Tongai:
Sean Lowe
Esther Fleece
Chad Robichoux
Ryan Reiss
Rudy Kalis
Jason Castro

Parker Young:
Beth/TJ
Michael/Tiffany

Trey Hill:
Stephen Baldwin

Justyna Fijalska:
David and Tamela Mann
Jessica Long
Danny Gokey
Mike Fisher/Carrie Underwood
Michael Ketterer
Remi Adeleke

Contents

CONTENTS

In Search of **Friendship**

Introduction

Love is the answer.

Whatever question you're asking or struggle you're dealing with, love is what you need.

Not the butterflies-in-your-stomach type of love that dies with the first frost of winter. But the stubborn, relentless kind of love that doesn't give up at irreconcilable differences, that sees past failure and annoyance, that holds on through storms.

"Love" may be easy to say, but the real thing can't be coded or typed. Love is not a "like" or a heart-shaped emoji. It can't be measured by retweets or followers, but rather by its stubbornness in difficulty, kindness in times of need, and grace in moments of weakness.

If you're surrounded but alone, "liked" but unloved, continually sending the world your message but feeling always unheard, then you need the stories in this book. If busyness has taken the place of connection and if virtual friends have replaced real ones, then these stories of genuine love are for you. If it's been a week since you did anything that let you connect, let you feel care and concern, then you need these stories.

Millions just like you have come to I Am Second seeking a place to belong, to be truly liked and heard. We are a movement that began as a website and a handful of films but has grown into an organization that brings hope and belonging to countless lonely people through the raw, beautiful, broken human stories of people just like you.

Thirty-six percent of the people you're liking online say they have no close friends they could turn to for help and support. Nearly half say they sometimes or always feel alone. One in three struggles with anxiety and worry.[1] If you are one of these people, then these stories of hope, love, and belonging are for you.

You are loved—even if you don't feel it. You are liked—even if you haven't seen a thumbs-up in weeks. A community is here for you, a people ready to say, "You are one of us."

"You belong" is the message of this book. "You are loved" is its anthem. In these pages you'll discover broken hearts healed, broken homes rebuilt, and broken lives resurrected.

The people here didn't find love on an app or a website. They didn't earn it, buy it, trade for it, or make themselves into someone who deserved it. They each found love only when they realized that God had found them.

Some had known that Jesus holds the secret of love but feared he wouldn't give it to them. Others never knew that Jesus cares about anything other than a person's politics or lifestyle. But they all discovered that love, belonging, and friendship begin in the understanding that the God of the universe came to earth because he loved them—and loves them!—specifically and personally.

And he loves you too.

in search of Love

Love is relentless.

It is many other things, of course. Love is patient and kind. It is generous and humble. It befriends truth and not evil. It forgives, protects, and trusts. But none of these other qualities would matter if they didn't last. Love that gives up is just heartbreak. Love that is faithful today but not tomorrow is empty and lonely. True love doesn't give up. It is relentless.

Pain comes when we think we have found love but really have found a broken version of it. The world is full of such fractured facsimiles: broken families, broken relationships, broken promises or expectations. The pain of such brokenness always corresponds to the amount of wholeness we expected. That's why the biggest hurts come from those we expect to love us the most.

The people in the following five stories lived with that kind of hurt. They grew up in troubled homes, lost a spouse, or struggled with singleness. All had their own troubles, but they also had a keen understanding that they needed real, lasting, and relentless love. They didn't need any more heartbreak. What they needed was someone who could love them forever.

And they all found it in the same Person.

Chapter 1

Legacy

breaking off
the past

DAVID AND TAMELA MANN, ACTORS AND ARTISTS

Nobody gets married expecting divorce. And nobody has children hoping to raise them in a broken home. And yet, approximately two in every five marriages (39 percent) will end in divorce.[1]

And what about the kids? While many seem to grow up relatively healthy despite the family discord, many others do not. Children of divorced parents face higher rates of social, emotional, and psychological troubles even into adulthood. They are more likely to struggle in their own future relationships and more likely to end up divorced themselves.[2]

That's a reality David and Tamela Mann have had to face and overcome. They each came from broken families and troubled childhoods, and their childhood struggles affected them both for years to come.

"Where I came from, you see a lot of physical and verbal abuse," David Mann says. While most parents fear some stranger hurting their child, the vast majority of child abuse involves a parent or relative.[3] Even more than divorce, such abuse-related trauma sticks with a person deep into adulthood.

"For me to not be that person, that's God's grace for me," David says. "Many people become a product of their environment. You become a statistic. I was determined not to become that, but I almost did."

Actor, stand-up comedian, and gospel singer David Mann is best known for his roles in Tyler Perry's *Meet the Browns* and *Madea Goes to Jail*. He and his wife, Tamela, also starred in their own popular comedy series, *Mann and Wife*. In each episode this couple and their cast of television children overcame whatever challenges life could throw at them. Inevitably their love won through. But David comes from a family very different from the one he portrayed on television.

"I never felt like I was good enough growing up," he says. "I always struggled with insecurity. The seed of that comes from growing up and not getting that time you need as a kid. Nobody said, 'I'm proud of you.'"

David's father left early in his life. His mother worked multiple jobs to keep food on the table and also fell into a series of destructive relationships. The paternal absence burned a hole in his confidence and self-esteem. The violence and verbal abuse he witnessed in his home compounded these struggles.

"Let's start with three-year-old me," he says. "That is when I first saw my mom abused. Imagine seeing your mom abused because she didn't cook what her man asked her to cook."

Little David vowed to himself never to let anyone hit his mother again. There's not much that a three-year-old can do, of course, but something inside of him hardened. He promised himself he would protect his mother no matter what it took.

"That's where the vicious little boy began," he says. "I flipped the switch. There was no turning it off after that. That does something to a kid. No kid should have to deal with that."

As David got older, his inner rage grew and extended to any and every male relationship. It poisoned any connection with a father figure or mentor. He couldn't trust again. He'd seen too much. The men in his life beat their women and yelled trash at them. If that's what it meant to be a man, then he'd have nothing to do with men.

"I was that vicious dude," he says. "I wasn't afraid of anybody. It didn't matter if you were six hundred pounds or sixty pounds. It ruined every relationship I had with men."

When another man beat his mother years later, David attacked him, determined to seek his own vengeance on him.

"I tried to kill him for messing with my mom," David says. "It was nothing but the grace of God that he didn't die."

Even after David married the love of his life, Tamela, the rage burned on. Tamela woke up her husband many nights because the anger followed him into his dreams. He fought and flung his arms in fits of fury while he slept. He defended his mother whether awake or asleep.

"I would literally wake up night after night shaking, fighting, tormented," he says. "Tamela said I had to do something about it. I had to get help. But who could I trust?"

Tamela brought her own set of baggage into the marriage. She was born the youngest of fourteen children and the only one from a different father. Being light-skinned when all her siblings were dark marked her as visibly different.

"I was the light sheep of the family," she says with a smile. "And I was always a thick girl. There were fat jokes. I had to develop a tough skin early on. I don't think they understood the feeling of being different, having the separation of looking different from everybody else in the family."

Tamela didn't know her father, though she did meet him once. He managed to pat her head but gave her no hug and no kiss. He seemed indifferent and uninterested. She never had a father who would ask about her day or tell her she was beautiful and important.

"I never felt really wanted," she says. "The spirit of rejection was there. My stepfather filled in some gaps, but then he got sick and died when I was twelve. The person I thought was about to be what I needed as a father was snatched. I drifted off as I got older, dabbling in the wrong things."

For a time music gave Tamela an escape. Her explosive voice would later earn her two Dove Awards and a Grammy, plus the 2014 BET Award for Best Gospel Artist. She would sing alongside Kirk Franklin, Mary J. Blige, Bono, and others. But before the career and all the awards, there was church. And church was what saved her.

"I found something I could call my own," Tamela remembers. "I wasn't a great reader. I didn't have a car. We didn't have money to be spending on a bunch of playtime with my friends. But church was free. Singing was free. Rehearsal was free. As long as I could find my way there, I could sing."

Singing, in turn, brought Tamela to God at age eight. She didn't discover him in a sermon or Bible study, but in a song. Her church music group was working on James Cleveland's classic arrangement of "I Don't Feel No Ways Tired." "I don't believe He's brought me this far to leave me," she sang from the song's bridge.[4] The song spoke of the many troubles that God is faithful to bring a person through. She had no context for much of what she was singing, but there was something in the words nonetheless.

"It gave me so much conviction," she recalls, "even at the age of eight. I really hadn't been through much, but I would weep at singing this song. I was speaking into my own life at an early age that God didn't bring me this far to leave me."

The conviction she discovered in music carried her through the doubts that came as she grew up. When other people went to parties, she went to church to sing her songs.

"It became life for me to open my mouth and make a joyful noise."

Despite the joy Tamela discovered in singing, she began noticing something about her friends—something that troubled her.

"I started seeing them having boyfriends," she says. "I didn't have one, me being a big girl."

Why didn't boys want to be with her? Was there something wrong with her? No, she wasn't thin, but did that really matter?

She asked herself these questions and more. She had guy friends, but they didn't want to be seen with her. Nobody gave her the attention she thought she deserved.

"It got to the point where I could be friends with a guy, but it was only in the shadows," she says. "It was hidden. They'd see me only in the evening time, when nobody knew about it. I felt like the shadow chick."

About that time Tamela's mother remarried. The family had been poor, but they'd always had food and the lights had stayed on. This changed with the new marriage. A new kind of stress entered their home.

"We thought it was going to be better when Mom remarried," Tamela says, recalling the financial stress of a single-parent home. "But it got worse. We were going behind grocery stores into the dumpsters to get food. It went from a wholesome home to a hectic one. He never hit my mom, but he was so mean. I could hear him fussing at her through the walls."

Like her future husband, David, Tamela changed after that. Seeing her mother mistreated brought bitterness and anger to her heart.

"I always had to bite, to lash out," she says. "I had to have the last word. I had to protect myself. I left home to get away from it. And it took me a while going into my marriage with David to let my guard down. He couldn't tell me anything. It took me a while to learn I could be loved and receive help. I didn't have to do it on my own."

The love Tamela found in her relationship with David was real . . . and powerful. Though his past brought out anger toward men, David had nothing but gentleness for his woman.

"I see greatness in her," he says. "Nobody can love my woman like I love my woman. I believe I was brought here on earth to bring the best out of her and make her every dream come true."

"He was the only person who didn't treat me as the shadow chick," Tamela says. "He liked me for me. To him I was precious enough to be in the light. He helped me see that I could be loved."

David and Tamela's relationship began a cycle of healing for both of them. David loved and valued Tamela, and she gave it all back to him. But nearly a decade into marriage, David still hadn't solved his problem relating to men. He found himself sabotaging every male relationship. He just couldn't let go of his past, couldn't shake the images of those men beating his mother. Even when he felt God tugging at him, prying his heart away from the hatred, he kept holding on to his anger.

"I knew he was telling me that there's really good men out there," he remembers, "but I fought it. He had a destiny for my life, but I would need to trust men to get there."

Then a day came when David was asked to speak at a seminar for a group of men. He came prepared with a talk and a topic. But when he got up to speak, something else came out.

"I hate all y'all," he told the crowd. Something in him just broke open. For so long he had stuffed his hatred and his anger behind a dam in his heart. And that day, in front of that room of men, God busted it open. Out came all the hatred, the anger, and the bitterness he had so long stuffed away.

"I don't trust any of you," he continued. "Not because of what you did to me, because of what you did to my mom,"

Even as he spoke, he could see the absurdity of his own thinking. He tried to hold his words back, but they just kept spilling out. Tears flowed.

David said things in front of all those men that he hadn't even been able to admit to himself. He told them his story about the violence he'd witnessed growing up. He admitted that he blamed every man for the nights he spent punching the air. Men had taken the happiness from his home. Men had stolen his peace and his security.

David's confession before that group of men was raw and painful. But in trusting them with it, he discovered the first step toward healing.

"When you feel true deliverance, it's like a weight that's taken off of you," he says. "Something just broke off of me that day. Ordinarily I would have wanted to fight the whole room. But that day I received true deliverance."

Confession is an act of trust. To confess you must first trust the people to whom you confess. You have to trust they won't throw hate back at you. You have to believe they will still love you after they see your ugliness. Until that day David never had the strength to make that leap. But once he did, he saw a whole new purpose for his life.

"I started on the path," he says. "I realized what the Lord had for me. My story could help men like me. I don't have to hate. I can help."

God did, indeed, have big plans for the Mann family. It was shortly after this that David and Tamela Mann won repeated roles in Tyler Perry's famed Madea productions. Tyler Perry's character, Madea, is an elderly, overbearing, and zany African American matriarch. But in his more than two dozen productions, including plays, films, and television shows, Madea and her cast of supporting characters inspire forgiveness, respect, and above all the love of family. David and Tamela's portrayal of two of those characters, Mr. Brown and Cora, eventually won them their own spin-off, Tyler Perry's *Meet the Browns*, which ran for 140 episodes. *Mann and Wife* and a reality series featuring the Mann family followed.

David and Tamela Mann have not achieved all their success because of who they are but because of who God made them to be. They are more than the sum of their upbringing. God took two lonely, angry people from broken families and made them into a beacon of joy and peace.

"We come from humble beginnings," David says, "basically nothing. To put these two people together with the insecurities that we have and then to thrive in our marriage for thirty years—that's nothing but grace. I wouldn't say Jesus is a part of my life. I would say Jesus *is* my life. It was nobody but Jesus that got me through that torment."

Nobody gets everything they need from their parents. Even the most stable home and most loving parents can't meet that mark. No matter what kind of home you came from, God has the answer for what you need. He specializes in bringing strength out of weakness and wholeness out of brokenness.

When Jesus came to this earth, he was born to an unwed refugee mother. When he picked his disciples, he chose twelve ordinary men. He didn't look for the wellborn, well positioned, or well educated. He found fishermen and tax collectors. He took the ordinary and made them *extra*ordinary. He took what the world threw away and used them to change the world.

That's the kind of plan he has for you too. He has a path for everyone, a plan for turning the bad into good, the dark into light. You just have to trust him with your life. You can submit to the inevitable failings of your upbringing, background, or past, or you can trust God to make more of it. But only one of those options will let you experience the kind of love and belonging you were meant to have.

Jason Castro of *American Idol* fame came from a very different kind of family. It wasn't his past that he struggled to trust God with but his future. God was about to ask him to walk away from all his dreams. But could he trust God with the road ahead?

Chapter 2

Dreams

daring to trust

JASON CASTRO, SINGER AND SONGWRITER

It's been more than a decade since Jason Castro's famous dreadlocks and captivating rendition of Leonard Cohen's "Hallelujah" won over millions on *American Idol*. He even managed to impress the famously sour Simon Cowell in season seven of the hit talent show. By then the show had already launched the singing careers of Kelly Clarkson, Carrie Underwood, and Chris Daughtry, to name a few. But Jason had none of those expectations.

At the time *American Idol* was at the height of its original fifteen-season run. (It briefly left the air in 2016, only to return two seasons later, adding even more years to its marathon run.) The show has spawned countless spin-offs and a whole category of reality television shows featuring aspiring artists and brooding judges. But all that was still in the future when Jason auditioned for the show. He signed up on a whim when the show came through his hometown of Dallas.

"I didn't expect much from that audition," Jason admits. "But I kept getting sent to the next round."

What surprised Jason the most was how this success came just after he'd given up on going anywhere with his music.

"I dreamed about being a lot of things growing up," he says. "I wanted to be a fireman one year, an astronaut the next. I wanted to be a paleontologist in fourth grade because of a dinosaur project we did. But by fifth grade, music came to the forefront."

For his birthday that year, Jason got his first instrument, a set of drums. By the age of sixteen he knew he wanted to make music his life. Even when he went to college, he continued playing drums for an aspiring rock band called Charlemagne. But college brought new challenges—and a big decision.

Jason graduated high school as a National Hispanic Merit Scholar and from there won an engineering scholarship to Texas A&M University. And up to that point he'd always balanced his academics with his musical ambitions. But the rigors of a college-level engineering degree quickly blew past his expectations.

"Engineering was not going to let me play in a band," he says, looking back. In his first semester, he realized that engineering degrees and rock bands don't easily mix.

"I dropped that major about a week into school," he says. But the reduced class load and change of major still left him struggling to keep up with his studies.

"I was playing in this band, traveling back and forth from Dallas to College Station, where my school was. I was not doing good in school at all."

Between rehearsals and playing out-of-town gigs, Jason never seemed to have the time to focus on his books, and his grades continued to sag. Many of his scholarships were tied to a certain

GPA, which he was no longer achieving. By the end of his first year, he lost many of his scholarships.

"I was embarrassed to go back to my parents and tell them," he says. "Tests had always been really easy for me. I'd never had to study in my life. I thought it would be the same in college. But I did poorly that year."

Jason's band hadn't yet made it, but neither was he making it at college. He saw a crossroads. He couldn't continue to split his attentions. He could do college, or he could do the band, but he couldn't do both. And he had begun to suspect that God was calling him to leave the band behind.

Since he got that first drum set so many years ago, music had grown to be a part of who Jason Castro was. It had become an identity. It was the way he engaged with the world and viewed his future. If he let that go, who would he be? Besides, the band also had grown increasingly serious, even to the point of talking to various labels. He'd be letting down his bandmates if he stepped away now.

"Music was my dream," he says. "But I felt like God was testing me. The guys in the band were all my friends. I loved music. But I wanted to make sure, whatever I did, that it fit into God's plan."

God has a way of boiling out life's distractions, of making clear what really matters. He pushes his people to make first things first and second things second. He has a plan for each person, but life is full of good but distracting opportunities. Even the best things in life, like friends or a fulfilling career, can off-ramp you to a life less than what God has planned.

Jason knew this about God, but he struggled with making the choice. What would happen if he did what he thought God wanted, leaving his band and his dream of making music? But God gave him only that one step. He didn't say where to go next or where Jason would go in the future. God was calling him to trust his plans without even knowing what those plans would be. Jason had to let go of his own plans and take a leap into the darkness.

He thought of another man who also had been sent out on an unknown path. God appeared to a man named Abram and told him to leave his family, his country, and all he knew and to go on a journey. God didn't tell Abram where to go, how long the journey would take, or any of the twists and turns he'd face along the way. He just said, "Go to the land I will show you."[1] From there Abram had to just trust—not in a particular vision for his life but in God himself. He had to just step out on that unknown path and trust that God knew where he needed to go.

For Abram the test lasted decades. He wandered with his wife, Sarai, out into an unknown place. They were given a promise that they would one day receive a home, a land, and a child and that Abram would be the "father of many nations."[2] But while they were waiting for that promise to be fulfilled, old age crept upon them. The thought of having a baby this late in life became a laughable concept, but God had promised it. He'd promised them a home in a foreign land and a child. And though Abram at the age of ninety-nine and his wife of ninety had neither, they chose to trust in the absurd, the impossible, and the ridiculous. That trust paid off. Abram and Sarai did become parents, and they settled in the land their descendants would one day claim as their own. God even gave them new names—Abraham and Sarah—to signal where their trust in God's plan had led them.

Jason Castro chose to follow Abraham's example and follow where God seemed to be leading him. He would let his long-held dream of being a musician go. He decided to return to school and trust God for what came next.

"My hope was set in something else now," he says. "My identity was not in what I might become, but in Jesus, in the Son of God."

It was the following year that everything aligned to bring Jason to an *American Idol* audition. The show came to his hometown while he was on break from school. The rules had just changed to let contestants compete with an instrument. And the new rule was just what Jason needed to audition successfully.

When Jason left Charlemagne, he'd discovered that drums just don't work well without a band. So he'd picked up a guitar and started singing and writing songs. If he hadn't followed God's leading, he would have still been on drums and not singing at all.

"I had only been playing guitar for a year or two at that point," he remembers. "But I'd never sung without it. I didn't even think I could. And really, I was uneasy with the whole music thing. From the beginning I'd had the attitude that if it was God's will, he would open the door. So I almost didn't go when the day came to audition. When I gave up the band, I'd felt like I was really giving up something that I loved, so that time in between was like a desert. There were a lot of lonely nights, a lot of tears. But all I gave up, God gave back tenfold."

Jason's audition went well. He made it to the live show, where his warm vocals and pared-down guitar stylings earned him a loyal base early on. Those fans stuck with him through a fourth-place finish on *American Idol*, edged out by David Cook, David Archuleta, and Syesha Mercado. Shortly afterward Jason released a record that reached number 18 on the Billboard 200 chart. But while the thirty million people who tuned in that season saw Jason fight to be America's next singing sensation, many of his battles stayed off camera.

"I found myself more and more in a lonely, lonely place," he says. "I really hadn't established a close group of friends since leaving the band. My mom and dad were really the core relationships I had during that time. I'd get like a hundred texts and phone calls a day, but more from acquaintances. They weren't friends on a deep level asking me how I was really doing.

"My biggest struggle was staying close to God. At first it was easy to get up early and read some Scripture, have some prayer time. But it just got so busy and so exhausting that it was hard to do that."

During this time Jason started dating Mandy, a girl he knew from high school. He proposed the following year. But Jason carried a secret into their relationship from his time with *American Idol*. The secret grew until it nearly cost him the relationship.

"This has been a big secret, an awkward secret," he admits.

It began with the pressure of being away from friends and family. As the loneliness took its toll on him, he began to lean back on an old habit of his. "I hate saying this," he confesses. "It's embarrassing. But I was addicted to pornography. I wasn't prepared for what the internet had. It started out small, but it just kept growing. By the time I was on the tour, it was every day."

"I felt really stagnant," he remembers. "I would try to read the Bible, but I was stuck in place. This addiction became the biggest thing in my life. It took away from everything. It was putting me down and keeping me depressed."

The shame of that addiction kept him up at night. But then the lack of sleep and the loneliness of the tour put him back in a place where he'd fail again. And the cycle of shame and addiction continued, each round making him ever more vulnerable to failing again. He felt trapped.

"It's this addictive cycle," he explains. "Once you do something, you think, *Well, I've already done it. I've already screwed up. Let's just keep going.* I couldn't stop."

But an even graver threat to his relationship with Mandy came when he let his online addiction turn into an offline encounter.

"I slept with someone I barely knew," he admits. "I did something I hadn't even come close to doing with my girlfriend. We barely had kissed."

The secrets piled up. Jason's fiancée didn't know about the pornography and certainly didn't know about the other incident. The guilt and the shame began to consume him.

"Having a secret just eats at you," he says. "I felt like a liar the whole time I was around Mandy. I was trying to have fun, but really I couldn't have fun because I had wronged her."

Jason kept the secret for months. But with each phone call, every visit, the weight of the secret grew and grew. Eventually it became more than he could bear.

"That's when I told her," he says. "It brought lots of tears. I told her I understood if she didn't want to stay with me."

Though Mandy initially ended the engagement, after four months apart she called to reconcile. They set a date, and on January 2, 2010, they married. But she threatened that if Jason ever looked at pornography again, she would divorce him.

"I won't ever look at it again," he committed. He installed

porn-blocking software on his devices and figured the battle was over and done. After all, he'd married the girl of his dreams. They were in love. What need did he have for his old habit?

"But I found myself looking at it again," he admits. And after Mandy's threat, he was even more reticent to tell her. He wondered how he could deal with his recurring addiction without talking with his wife about it. How could he get help if he couldn't disclose the secret?

The cycle of shame returned as before. Jason fell ever deeper into darkness and a sense of despair. Their relationship grew distant.

Eight months into the marriage, a friend invited Jason and Mandy to a support group at their church. Neither knew what to expect, but they agreed to attend, thinking that maybe it could help their marriage. As they took their seats, someone read aloud a list of "steps." Without knowing it, they had stepped into a twelve-step program.

"Mandy just started crying," he says. "She'd just never pictured her life like this."

What followed was a series of stories. People in the group began sharing their personal struggles with addiction and the damage that had resulted. The stories were shocking, even depressing, but also refreshingly honest.

"They were so down and seemingly hopeless," Jason remembers. "But by the end of the meeting I couldn't help but be filled with hope. God used people sharing their struggles to reveal to me and all of us this sense of hope. That's how it works."

Jason and Mandy returned to the group again and again and continued to find inspiration in the honesty and truthfulness they heard there. Despite the hardships the people shared and the difficulties their addictions had caused, everyone could sense hope in having others know them for who they really were. The fifth step in the twelve-step process involves this very thing—confession, admitting to God, ourselves, and another person what we have done. Letting the secret out positions a person for healing. Nothing else can happen until honesty has its way.

After attending the twelve-step group for nearly two months and listening to others' stories, Jason finally decided to share his own struggle. He stood up in front of the group—his wife included—and confessed his pornography problem. He didn't know if Mandy would still love him after that. But he also realized that she couldn't really love him *until* he confessed everything. How could she love a man she didn't really know?

Up to that point, she had only loved the Jason he let her see. But would she love the real Jason? That was the question he now sought an answer for.

"After that, everything began to change," he says. "I started to feel freer. I always believed in God, but I didn't really trust him with everything. I thought this was too dark to share with anybody. But once I trusted him with this, I started down the road of living a godly life, being known. It feels good to be known."

Jason took drastic steps in his subsequent road to recovery. He got rid of his cell phone and any device that could access pornography. He made a radical commitment to transparency. The people in the twelve-step group became his community and place of confession.

Jason knows now that if he feels temptation and doesn't share it with anybody, then it's only a matter of time before he succumbs. So now he confesses even the smallest hint of temptation to his support group and to Mandy. This policy of openness has allowed him to find strength in others and support through his addiction. It has also grown a new channel of trust in his marriage.

"That's the real miracle," he says. "I'm able to have a family, be married to my wife, and us to have a better relationship than either of us ever imagined. I've done some things, but I'm able to be free of those things because of Jesus Christ. Now I'm a free man."

Jason's story began with an act of trust. God told him to step out from what he knew and go down an unknown road. He fretted, he cried, he wondered, but in the end he decided to also trust. Then, as his journey continued, Jason learned that trust is an essential ingredient of love. When you trust someone, you open up to them. You let that person really know you. Trust is in the foundation of every great relationship, whether it's with a spouse or with God.

That's the reason confession is always a foundational step in a relationship with God. It's not a matter of information, but a matter of trust.

After all, God already knows everything we've done, everything we are going to do, and everything we are doing and thinking right now. He has also promised to forgive us anything and everything if we come to him. So he doesn't need our confession to tell him something he's not aware of or to give him an excuse to rain down fiery darts of punishment. What he cares about is this: Do we trust him enough to tell him everything?

That's the same struggle Esther Fleece had, though she wasn't hiding an addiction or an affair or anything she had done. Her entire childhood was her secret, and she kept it buried beneath a smile that hid the pain—until she couldn't keep it hidden anymore.

Chapter 3

Stalker

when love goes bad

ESTHER FLEECE, AUTHOR

For many people, college is a chance to spread their wings.

For Esther Fleece, it was an opportunity to escape her life. Or so she hoped.

"College was a place where people didn't know your past," she says. "They just knew who you were in the present. I felt like I came into my own in those years. I had a lot of friends, and I was involved in a lot of activities. I loved it so much because I felt like I could forget my past."

As a child, Esther Fleece hadn't understood what was happening to her family. She'd felt like a normal kid in a normal family living in a normal neighborhood, going to school and church like all the other kids she knew. But then it all started to change. She began noticing bruises on her mother. Her father's temper became worse and their relationship started to change. She could see the terror in her mother's eyes whenever his yelling began. The violence and threats would escalate until she and her mother had to flee to a nearby hotel.

"We'd go to Salvation Army in the morning to pick out clothes for the next day of school," she recalls. "The police would come, but nothing seemed to change. The police came to our house so frequently that I thought they were friends with my dad."

It was only later that Esther connected these visits with the bruises on her mother. But eventually she witnessed the violent episodes firsthand. "My hero was becoming the most unsafe man I had ever been around. I loved my dad. I loved my mom. I loved my family. But we were becoming really unsafe."

Normal is always whatever you grow up with. Uncertainty and violence became her normal. This made her build walls between herself and others. She refused to let anyone get close to her and she fought them away if they tried. She feared the possibility of more hurt and disappointment.

Eventually the police did more than just give warnings. The length of her father's prison stays would vary, but the same pattern held. The police would come and arrest him, then he'd get out, and the destructive cycle would begin again.

"I was always summoned for the court cases," she remembers. "I would have to sit in a room by myself, and nobody explained to me what was happening. Then I would have to walk into a courtroom with both of my parents, one on each side of the room. I was supposed to tell the story of our home life. Both of my parents hurt and neglected me. But in the courtroom I would have to pick who I was going to say nicer things about so I wouldn't get hurt more when I went home. It was just awful."

Each time the lawyers and the judges gave her impossible choices. She had to choose which version of home to reveal, which parent to favor. But she went home to pain and instability no matter the choice.

When her father would get out of jail, he'd attempt love and care, but the reality was obsession and danger. "He thought he was rescuing me," she remembers. "I'd never get a warning when he was being released from jail. He would just be released. Then he would fixate on me. At first I thought that was because I was his daughter and he wanted to be with me. But he was dangerous. He tried kidnapping me numerous times. Whenever he was around, there was always chaos."

Esther and her mother began moving from house to house. In each place Esther was forced to find a new group of friends, adjust to a new school, and hope for peace and safety. "I was having to make new friend groups every year," she recalls. "People asked why we'd moved, but how could I answer that? We were hiding. That was the truth—but you didn't share those things."

Her mother eventually divorced her father and remarried, but the relationship ended poorly. "He ended up having an affair," Esther remembers. "And I was the one who found out about it."

Esther's stepfather left after she told her mother about the infidelity. She thought he'd be gone for an hour. When he didn't come back, she thought maybe it would be for a day. But he never returned. He just left and that was it.

"That's when my mother began hating me," she says. "There I was, fourteen years old, and everyone had left me. My dad was unsafe. My stepdad found somebody better, a better family. And now my mom didn't want to be my family anymore. I would go home sometimes and the locks would be changed. It was like I wasn't welcome in my own home. I was left to make it through this world on my own. I continued my way in school to the best of my ability, but I didn't tell anyone there what I was going through."

School had always been a refuge for her, a place of safety. Relationships had always been the opposite. Those who claimed to love her the most had hurt her the most. Love had proved too dangerous. So she decided to close herself off and start new at college.

"I hated the word *love*," she says. "I would hear it in church. I would hear people say, 'God loves you.' And they would say it like everything was fine, like we should just think that's a good thing. But the love I understood was full of violence and hate. If God was going to love me like that, no thanks. I didn't want God to love me. I didn't want love at all."

College gave Esther the opportunity to forget all this pain. She was desperate to shape a new life and a new identity. So she decided to just leave her past in the past.

"I never set out to be fake," she says. "I wanted a different story. I would share just enough of my past to satisfy people and go about the rest of my day. I decided I would just pretend to be fine. I continued on this path of faking being fine. I became the girl that had it all together."

She projected this image of having no baggage and no buried secrets, but the cost was authentic connection with others. People at school and church assumed she was fine. But she wasn't.

Staying busy was Esther's salvation in those days. "As long as I stayed working fifteen hours a day and took twenty-one credit hours at school, then I didn't have to think about the brokenness," Esther says. She signed up for everything she could think of—more hours at work, more classes, more church events, and more extracurricular activities. "I joined cheerleading teams and played varsity sports," she remembers. "I didn't have to think about my past if I kept busy. I wanted to live only in the present."

Actually, though, this pattern of busyness and escape had started many years earlier, after her parents' divorce. "I ran for class president or vice president each year from middle school into college," she remembers. "I stayed for after-school and church activities whenever I could. It meant I didn't have to go home. I never wanted to go home."

As Esther grew into adulthood, she managed a new kind of normal. She continued to battle the nightmares, the fears, and the memories of the past, but she painted over all of them. She pretended it all away. She completed school and spent the next fifteen years building a successful writing, speaking, and professional career. Then just as the memories of her childhood began loosening their grip, her father—who had been absent from her life for decades—reappeared.

"When he showed up, twenty years after he left our family, I physically couldn't go home," she recalls. "There was no telling what his intentions were. I had to live with another family. I took out restraining orders, all of which were violated."

Worst of all, the emotional torment and fear from her childhood came roaring back.

"I'm a grown woman and feel like I'm four years old sometimes," she says. "I'm an accomplished woman, but I can still go back and fear for my life like a child."

The stalking continued. Esther was fleeing from home to home again, just as she'd had to do as a child, living out of a suitcase. Her dad left notes on her car and the steps of her house. He even showed up at her workplace.

Finally, in the midst of this frightening and unstable existence, Esther decided to meet with a counselor, who worked to crack open the facade she had built.

Brick by brick, she had enclosed herself away from feeling, from love, and from recognizing the reality of what she had suffered. She'd kept herself busy and occupied. But she had reached a point where the coping mechanisms had ceased to work. The counselor pushed her to simply recognize the pain of her past and to let herself mourn.

"I wanted to forget it all," she says, "but I couldn't. Being performance driven didn't work anymore. I got to the point where I didn't even want to get out of the bed in the morning. The nightmares were terrible."

"You have never grieved what has happened to you," her counselor said. "You've never grieved for yourself. You've never grieved your abuse or your abandonment. You can't move forward unless you grieve."

When the one-hour counseling sessions didn't work, the counselor had Esther come in for three or four hours at a stretch. He called these long sessions "intensives."

"This is so dumb," Esther would think. "Why should I force myself to feel these things? Why am I paying money to feel these things?"

"For so long I had pretended that everything was fine," she says. "Nobody would know what I went through. But now I was sharing all this with my counselor. I started experiencing for the first time these emotions that I had run from and suppressed. I finally got the courage to deal with them. I didn't think what he was telling me made any sense, but I was being pulled out of this pit of shame. It was the most painful, muddy, gross pit you can think of. But I really had to deal with reality. I couldn't fake it anymore, couldn't pretend my life was okay. My life had never been okay."

"I was unwanted," she realized. "I was unloved. I was neglected. I was abused. I was abandoned by every single family member."

The weight of all these realizations nearly crushed her. Thoughts of suicide came to mind. But still she managed to press forward, trying to find a way to live with her past.

"How do I feel the full weight of what happened to me and seriously forgive people?" she remembers asking herself. She could superficially forgive—slough off all her feelings and pretend nothing was wrong. But that never really lasted. And now she was really looking at the terrible reality of her childhood and all the people who should have loved and cared for her but who instead had abused and neglected her.

"I had to redefine what love is," she recalls. "I struggled. The only thing I knew about love was negative."

During this time, she found solace in the story of David from the Bible.

"I was hurting so badly," she remembers. "The only comfort that I had was reading the Bible. People can criticize the Word of God all they want, but for me it was a lifeline. It was literally all I had. I was being plagued by nightmares every single night. My life was a nightmare. I did not know how to function as a normal human being, but I found the story of David normalizing to me. It was the only thing that got me through those years."

One of the most famous names in the Bible, David is best known for his great poetry, for leading the nation of Israel as its most famous king, and for being a direct ancestor of Jesus. But those are just the highlights that people like to remember. The scars and hardships of his life are often forgotten, but they were what brought healing to Esther.

When David was a young boy, a prophet came to his town and anointed him the next king of Israel. But Israel already had a king, and that king already had an heir—a situation that would bring David much trouble.

In the years after the anointing, David did his best to serve his country and his king faithfully. He and the men he led defeated giants and overcame entire armies of adversaries[1]—all in service to his king. David rose in the ranks to be a general, serving with great skill and daring and earning the love of all the people. He even became close friends with the king's son. But the king, overcome with jealousy and increasingly unstable, grew to hate David and suspect him of treachery. Finally he made an attempt on David's life. When the attempt failed, he chased after David with all the resources he could muster.

Again and again David reminded the king of the goodness he had brought to his kingdom and of the valiant deeds he had done in the king's name. But the king never relented. The half-crazed king chased David to the very end of his days. Only after the king's suicide did David find safety and become king in his own right.[2]

Esther understood the injustice and the hatred that David faced. She didn't empathize with his victories or his heroism, but with his defeats. She identified with David when he fled his home again and again and hid in caves to escape the king.

For so long she had hated the story God had written for her life. Why must she suffer so much? But David had suffered too. His story had been full of pain, injustice, and struggle. Yet the Bible made it clear that God loved David dearly. He even called David "a man after my own heart."[3]

"I thought my biological father was going to take my life," she says. He stalked her wherever she fled, and she figured the next time he was out of prison or the next time he found her, her life could be over. If he found her, he would be there to render his twisted version of love.

Esther suspected David would resonate with that fear. "He was always running for his life from a crazy man who was supposed to be a father figure," she recalled from his story. She read David's poetry in the book of Psalms where he cries out to God, "How long, Lord? Will you forget me forever?"[4] and she heard her own voice in his.

That's when she knew that God understood her. She still didn't always understand his plans. She didn't know why he would allow all the evil in her life. But she saw the way he wove David's tragedy into victory and knew that God was someone she could trust. She found in him a better version of love—a love that remained good even when surrounded by evil. In the Bible she found a God who remained faithful even when the whole world abandoned her.

"I really have difficulty reading Scripture now and not seeing the hardship," she says. "I see the false imprisonments, false accusations, sorrow, shipwrecks, and I see that this is what people of God will go through. I used to think that if I did good things, then everything was going to be wonderful."

Instead, what she found was a God who promises strength through hardship, new life through death, and freedom at the other end of captivity. She discovered that God uses the hard things of this world to bring about even greater things in the next. He doesn't always deliver when and how we might want, but he always keeps his promises, and he never ceases to love.

"He is near to the brokenhearted," she says. "I used to think God is uninterested and uninvolved. I didn't think he liked me. But now I realize that I am serving a God who was broken. The Son of God was despised. He was killed. He did all that for me. It was like he did it all to say, 'I want to make you mine. I want to adopt you into my family and show you what love really is.'"

In time Esther learned to forgive her father, though she didn't get the happy ending she always wanted. Her family never reconciled. She lived for years looking over her shoulder, wondering if her father would find her again. But she learned she didn't have to hide her pain or pretend it doesn't exist. That God loves in good times and in bad. That he cares for her whether she smiles or cries.

And when she learned to open her heart to God, Esther learned to open her heart to love. Shortly after interviewing for this story, Esther made a commitment to love. In 2016, she married Joel Allen and started a family of her own. Her father died just five days after her wedding day.

God doesn't require us to smile for him in order to love us. He doesn't need us to pretend all is well when all is wrong. God doesn't need our lives all tidy and put together in order to care for us. And we don't need to pretend to be strong when we're feeling weak. After all, it was Jesus who said, "Come to me, all you who are weary and burdened, and I will give you rest."[5] God wants us to come to him no matter what we're going through. His promise is to never leave us or forsake us. Esther has found that he always keeps his promises.

Danny Gokey learned this lesson the hard way. He believed with all his heart that God would only let good things happen to the people he loved. So when bad things happened, he struggled to know if God had left him.

Chapter 4

Comeback

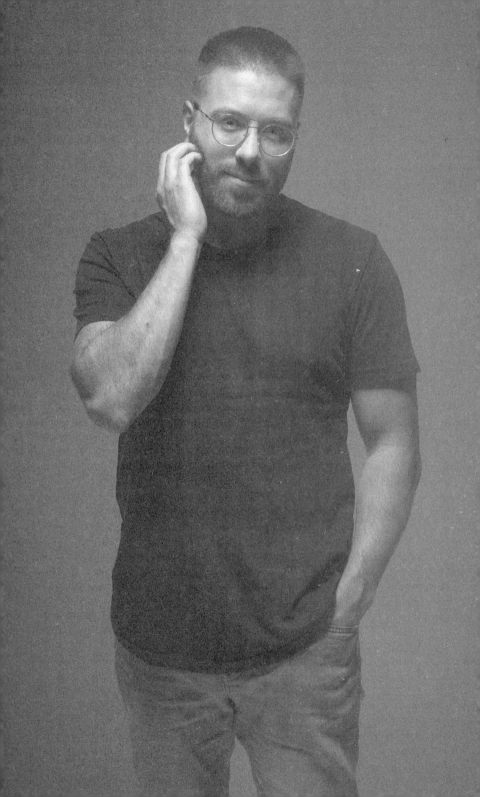

surviving the
ultimate loss

DANNY GOKEY, SINGER

"There was always this gnawing in the back of my mind," Danny Gokey says. "Is God with me? Or is God going to leave me because of my mistakes?"

Danny grew up in a Christian home. His grandfather was a pastor. His parents brought him to church every week. He learned the foundations of the faith while attending a Christian school. But throughout that time he constantly worried if God would save his soul in the end.

The message of Jesus is simple: "All the world is perishing. Jesus came to save it. Trust him and you will be saved. You will escape death and inherit heaven." And Danny never doubted that message. He just doubted his own ability to trust Jesus.

"I was one of those kids that would give my life to the Lord hundreds of times," he says. "I wasn't secure in what Jesus did for me."

So Danny Gokey worried. Had he done enough for God? Did he have enough faith? Could he prove that faith? He spent many years attempting to do just that.

"If I fall, does that mean I've lost my salvation?" he pondered with every mistake or mishap. "It gnawed at me. Fear was always this underlying thing in my life. But I just bottled it up."

He feared for his soul. Then he feared his fear. Was fear proof that he didn't have faith?

The fear compounded and multiplied. Speaking it aloud to others would only make it seem more real, he thought, so he kept it secret.

"I remember as a boy waking up at night with my head spinning with fear," he says. "I would wake up my dad and ask him to pray with me."

"What's wrong? What's going on?" his father would ask him.

"I would never tell him," he says. "I was scared to reveal what was going on in my head, the craziness of these thoughts."

His father would pray with him. He would comfort his son with Bible verses that promised peace and salvation. This would calm Danny for a time, but the fear would return. He found the same cycle happening at church. He would experience a closeness with God in church or at church events that made him feel better, but the fear would always return.

Danny's fears followed him into his high school years. That's when he met Sophia.

"We started going to a church together," he says. "I started learning new things about God. I started to learn about his character from the Bible."

By that time he had spent years feeling troubled and full of fear. But now, as he looked back, he saw that God had been with him the whole time. Throughout all the ups and the downs, God had walked with him. He'd feared all those many years that God would leave, but he never had.

One verse in particular stuck out to Danny:

> You will face all kinds of trouble. When you do, think of it as pure joy. Your faith will be tested. You know that when this happens it will produce in you the strength to continue. And you must allow this strength to finish its work. Then you will be all you should be.[1]

Danny could still sense fear wandering through the back of his head, but he had something to grip onto now. There was a purpose in his fight with fear. If Danny let him, God would bend this fear into strength.

"I learned to read the Scriptures," Danny remembers. "And God started downloading things and developing things in me. The only way you know the material that God has given you is to be tested."

Danny and Sophia both served at their church. She led the children's ministry. He led the worship team and worked in outreach to the needy.

"I remember the burning passion on the inside of me," he says. "I was working a ton of hours. I led the music at church.

I had a passion for the downcast and for those who don't have much. So I served at a ministry called Inner City Impact, where we would go out and feed the hungry and clothe those living on the streets."

By the time Danny and Sophia married in 2004, their lives seemed full and fulfilling. They had found a community to belong to and a new understanding of God that gave them peace. Danny's struggles with fear had subsided to the point that he believed God would do anything for him. He had come to trust God for all his needs and all his prayers.

But as his childhood battle with fear quieted, a new challenge emerged. Sophia had been born with a heart defect. She'd had surgery to fix it and never had any other problems. But then, a year into their marriage, Sophia's heart put her in the hospital. The doctors grew concerned when her heart started racing at two hundred beats per minute, more than twice the usual rate. The doctors insisted on surgery to fix what had been missed before.

Danny and Sophia were both twenty-four years old and felt far too young to be worrying about heart issues. They cried. They felt confused. They also felt afraid, but faith kept the fear at bay.

"We were determined to believe God for a miracle," Danny says. "We had seen supernatural things in our church. We'd seen God heal people, set people free, and deliver people from various things. We trusted God for his healing again."

They both determined not to let fear reign. They knew God. They knew his power, his love, and his ability to heal. Why wouldn't he heal two of his servants, two people who trusted and believed in him?

But Sophia's heart problems continued. She was in and out of the hospital and underwent multiple surgeries but still had no healing. But they kept on praying and believing. They posted faith-filled Scripture verses all around their apartment, even stuck one right on the mirror in the bathroom so they would be reminded of God's healing power as soon as they got up in the morning.

"You'd open up the refrigerator, and you'd see another Scripture passage," Danny recalls. "We had Scripture passages everywhere. We had belief. We had faith."

The day finally came for Sophia to have open-heart surgery. They had thought God would heal her before that became necessary, but now they would have to trust him to heal her through the surgery.

"God, why are we here?" Danny remembers praying at the time. "I thought you had all the power. I thought you could do all things."

He struggled to match the Jesus who healed the lame and raised the dead with the God who seemed to have done nothing for his wife. But still he chose to trust that God would heal his wife.

"The doctors said that even that surgery would only be a temporary fix," he says. "She would eventually need a heart transplant. They didn't know how long a life she would have."

The four-hour surgery stretched to eight hours due to complications. Then the doctors halted the procedure and informed Danny that they still hadn't been able to fix her heart. Sophia would need an artificial heart immediately and a transplant as soon as possible.

The medical team put Sophia on an artificial heart and added her to the transplant list. They started praying for a new heart. "We still believed that God was doing something in that moment," Danny remembers. He refused to let the fear of his childhood return in his life.

Danny returned to their apartment while Sophia rested at the hospital. As he prayed and waited, he heard the phone ring. "You need to get down here." The voice on the other end gave him a somber warning. "She's not going to make it. You need to come say good-bye."

The fear of falling from God's grace had plagued Danny Gokey as a child. In the end, would God grant him life or death? But in the years he had found new hope and peace. He had learned to trust a God who heals, forgives, and grants life. And he had trusted that God for his beloved Sophia. But now Sophia was dying, and Danny was distraught.

"The weight of the world just crushed on my shoulders," he says. "I remember us sitting at the hospital just begging and pleading and crying."

"God, you save her!" he yelled. "You have to heal her. You have to. You cannot leave me alone like this. You can't leave me."

"I had already struggled with this battle," he remembers. "Is God with me or is God not with me? That's what I kept asking myself."

Despite their prayers, Sophia passed away. Danny felt the fear rush back in. He had believed that if God was with him, then God would answer his prayers. But he had prayed so fervently for Sophia's healing, and Sophia had died anyway. Did that mean

God had left him? Was God mad about something he had done, some lack of faith? Was God now out to get him?

"I couldn't do anything for the funeral arrangements," Danny says. "My mom and her sisters had to do it. I felt such complete loss and numbness."

Sophia's burial was the end of his story, at least as far as he could tell. He feared God had left him. His life had gone from full to empty. He'd had a wife and a vibrant relationship with God, and now he had neither.

"I had a lot of disappointment," he remembers. "I had a lot of frustration. All the anger, the numbness, it clouded up my vision to see God. I thought in that moment it was the end of the story, but really it was the beginning of a new chapter."

Gradually an idea began to emerge through the fog. "We liked *American Idol*," he says. "And Sophia had wanted me to audition. And this year would be the last one I could audition before I aged out. So I had promised her I would do it."

Despite his heartbreak and loss, or perhaps because of it, Danny decided to keep his promise. It so happened that Sophia's death came only four weeks before the audition. Danny traveled to Kansas City still raw from his loss but determined to keep his promise.

"I remember standing in those lines with tears falling down," he says. "One moment I'm happy because this could be a possibility for something good. The other I'm wondering how I'm going to live this new chapter without her here.

"When you walk through loss or massive disappointment, it's easy for your perspective to get very, very small, to the point where you can only see the problem. But when I walked on to this TV show, in that moment, my perspective got so much bigger. God brought hope to my life through the most unlikely vehicle: Hollywood."

Danny walked out of his initial audition with unanimous support from all four judges and the golden ticket ushering him into the next round. He got a glimpse of what God could still have in store for him. "I saw hope for a future," he recalls. "But a month later a familiar friend came right back: fear.

"I fell into a such a deep depression," he recalls. "I was in such a darkness because of the pain and the disappointment. I felt like I was falling down and like none of it mattered. Hollywood week came, and I wasn't even sleeping at night because I was dealing with these debilitating thoughts again, wondering if God was with me."

Hollywood week would take the nearly 150 contestants who had received golden tickets in the auditions and winnow them down to just 36. After making it to the top 54, Danny's fear had spiraled to a point where he wanted to quit.

"I do not want to go on this TV show," he prayed, looking up to God. "I'm a mess. I'm going to look like a mess in front of all these people."

Danny had ridden the excitement of *American Idol* success for as long as he could. But the loss of Sophia still lingered fresh in his mind. He found himself facing ever-increasing waves of grief, doubt, and ultimately fear.

As a child, Danny had grown up hearing that basic message of salvation. He knew that Jesus came, died for all, and offered life to any who would trust him. But Danny still wondered if he had trusted God enough. It was in these dark moments, when his faith was tested, that he saw doubt creep out from his soul. He had faith in God, but he also had doubt. Could God accept him, would he still want him, if all Danny could offer was a feeble mix of faith and doubt? Was it enough?

He cried out for God, knowing he didn't have the strength on his own.

Be still. Danny felt the words come to his mind. *And know that I am God.*

This was a verse he had known all his life. It comes from a song contained in the book of Psalms that speaks of God being present even in the worst of calamities. It reads:

> The earth may fall apart.
>> The mountains may fall into the middle of the sea.
>> But we will not be afraid.
> The waters of the sea may roar and foam.
>> The mountains may shake when the waters rise.
>> But we will not be afraid. . . .
> "Be still, and know that I am God." . . .
> The LORD who rules over all is with us.[2]

Rather than proving his absence, tragedy is an opportunity to prove God's presence. This truth had escaped Danny all his life. He had thought the God of the universe always dealt out punishment for misdeeds and blessing for good behaviors. Dark times meant that God had left you and you were at fault. But God's word in his darkest hour was one of presence and comfort: "Be still."

"This verse has become a life lesson for me," Danny says. "It has had the most powerful impact on my life. It tells me to stop striving, stop fighting, and to let go. When I hang on to the pain of the past, the resentment or unforgiveness, these are the very things that will pull me down. When God gave me that verse, he was telling me to let go of all my questions about why he didn't heal Sophia. When I did that, when I let go, it was like someone took this cork out of my heart and all these negative emotions just flowed out. The bitterness that grew from the situation, the disappointments and the anguish—it just drained out."

Danny finished Hollywood week and passed through to the semifinals. He belted through round after round on the show without ever landing in the bottom two. It wasn't until the judges had to choose between Danny, Kris Allen, and Adam Lambert that he was eliminated.

"God put newness in my life," Danny relates. "Through the show he let me see how I have been able to share hope with so many people because they related to my story."

One message he received while on the show came from a woman who had been about to commit suicide. She'd actually been holding the gun in her hand when Danny came on. She'd heard him crying as he told his story about how he had found hope in God. Now she was writing to tell him that she, too, had decided to trust in God and had put the gun down when she heard him cry.

"God has given me a stronger faith and a foundation to say, 'It's not over yet,'" Danny says. "I've noticed this progression in every part of my life. There's always another chapter, even when I think the story is over. All I have to do is keep walking forward."

Danny has learned that God doesn't love you more when you do good or love you less when you do bad. When the worst happens, it doesn't mean his affections for you have changed. His offer to save is not based on a perfect outworking of faith or a list of laws that must be kept. God is God. Come hell, high water, or the death of your spouse, God still rules the universe. He has not forgotten his promises, and he will not leave you.

"There is something absolutely wrong with a works mentality," Danny says of those who, like himself, have sought to work their way into God's favor. "I burned myself out trying to do every aspect of works and keep every aspect of God's law. As a young kid I didn't believe Jesus was enough. I believed it was Jesus plus 'Now I've got to do x, y, and z.' But he is enough. He comes first. He is first. And I am second."

God loves you.

That's it.

He doesn't require you to clean up, act up, or 'fess up before he loves you. He loves first. Everything else comes later. His promise to save you flows from that love. Whatever heartbreak, disappointment, or loss you are facing, it's not God saying he doesn't love, but him saying "I am God. Be still and let me prove that I still love you."

Sean Lowe had to learn about God's love through loss too. But while Danny's loss occurred before he got on television, Sean Lowe had his broadcast to the world. The girl he loved broke his heart in front of everyone. That was not supposed to be God's plan for his life.

Chapter 5

Choices

single reality

SEAN LOWE, *THE BACHELOR* CONTESTANT

"Never in a million years did I think I would do a cheesy reality television show about love," Sean Lowe admits. The Texas native first stepped into the spotlight in 2012 as a contestant on *The Bachelorette*. He became a fan favorite to match with Emily Maynard, that season's featured single woman. But Sean had never actually applied to be on the show in the first place and certainly had never planned on falling in love on television.

"I got a call from a Los Angeles area code one day," Sean says. "I didn't recognize it. There was a girl on the other end. She told me she was with the casting department for *The Bachelorette*. And I had no idea what she's talking about. I thought it was a joke."

But it was no joke. Sean's sister had sent in a picture of her brother with her best pitch to have him on the show.

"I let the girl talk for about five minutes," he says. "But then I told her I had no desire to be on reality television. And I certainly didn't want to subject myself to all the public criticism that came with being on a show like *The Bachelorette.*"

What fans love about the show and of its long-running parent show, *The Bachelor,* is, well, all the love. Every season the show moves toward pairing two beautiful single people for happily-ever-after. Each episode the leading lady or man is wooed, romanced, and sought after by a cadre of possible lovers. As the weeks go by, potential mates are progressively passed over one by one until true love emerges with the season-finale marriage proposal. The contestants go from never-met to forevermore over the course of a ten-week season.

But critics have also voiced a steady chorus of criticism. Many have pointed out the overemphasis on beauty, charm, first impressions, or the gimmicky scenarios the contestants participate in. Can a person really find their true love like this? Is reality television really the best place for two people to make a decision like marriage? All this rushed through Sean's head as the recruiter talked with him about joining the show.

"Just think about it," she said. "You could travel, see the world, and meet some cool friends. Who knows? You might even fall in love."

"I told her not to hold her breath," he says. "But I agreed to think about it."

Sean had recently joined his family's insurance business. It was something he had sworn never to do. He hated the idea of the nine-to-five job, the cold calls, and the slacks he'd inevitably be forced to wear.

After college he'd had some big dreams and taken some big risks. He'd started a financial services company with investment money from some partners, hoping to make millions. But when a government regulation wiped away everything the company had sought to do, he'd lost everything. His investors wanted answers. He didn't have any they would like. They threatened to sue. Insurance became his escape.

"I had given it my honest effort," he says of his failed venture. "I did everything legally, but it was out of my control. I was afraid for my future. I had a lot of sleepless nights, so much anxiety and unrest. I needed to do something that would give me security. That's when I finally agreed to join my brother-in-law as an insurance agent."

He regretted the decision almost at once. He couldn't stand the mundane life he'd just signed up for. He wanted out—or at least a break—and the show might give him the excuse he had been looking for. The thought of escaping the humdrum world of insurance was enough to convince him to call the woman in the casting department back.

She told him she needed a video. He'd have to film himself describing his dream woman, his aspirations in life, and where he thought he'd be in ten years. He'd have to answer questions like "Do you want kids?" and "Describe your dating history" and "Do you have any special talents?" The tape would be played to the audience on the show, but it would also help inform the bachelorette whether he was the man for her.

I FOUND LOVE

Sean made the tape and sent it off. He went back to his nine-to-five job, still not sure if he wanted to be on the show. Then, a week later, the phone rang.

"Are you ready to pack your bags?" the woman in the casting department asked. The producers had loved his tape and wanted him on the show.

"At that point I was ready," he says. "I needed a break from insurance. I'd never thought I would be a part of something like this. But after thinking about it for a week or so, I thought, *I just want a free vacation.*"

So with the promise of some much-needed adventure, Sean flew out to meet bachelorette Emily Maynard.

The season opener took place in her hometown of Charlotte, North Carolina. Twenty-five suitors, including Sean, jostled for the opportunity to make an impression. The nineteen contestants who survived the opening cut moved into a sprawling mansion that provided the backdrop for the next several episodes.

On week three, Sean caught Emily's attention while on a group date that included twelve other suitors and a band of Emily's friends. As it turns out, shirtless push-ups can actually work. His first one-on-one date with Emily took place during week five, when the show moved to London. They kissed outside of Buckingham Palace, and for the first time Sean thought maybe the show could give him more than just an adventure. This could be where he found love.

I like being around her, he thought. *This is a girl that I would pursue if I met her back home under normal circumstances.*

Several more weeks went by, more of the men were sent home, but Sean remained.

"I spent more and more time with Emily," he says. "A couple more weeks go by. And I'm actually developing feelings for this girl on a reality TV show."

He could hardly believe it himself. He hadn't come on the show expecting to fall in love. He'd come more for the adventure than the romance. But now, with cameras all around, he found his heart surprisingly drawn to Emily.

"The whole time I'm staying in prayer," he says. "I ask for God's guidance, for him to direct me. And all signs were pointing toward this girl, Emily. There came a point where I thought I was going to spend the rest of my life with her. I could see myself being her husband. God was using this reality TV show to introduce me to my wife and my future daughter."

Early on, Emily had revealed she had a daughter. Several of the suitors would later exit the show after comments that showed their lack of excitement about the prospect of fatherhood. But Sean felt differently.

"I'd never contemplated being a father before," he said. "Marriage was a new idea for me. But after about six weeks of being on the show, I knew that I loved her and would spend the rest of my life with her." And he was even open to the idea of being a father.

The final weeks of the show brought the cast to the little country of Curaçao in the Caribbean. The week before, Emily had traveled home with each of the semifinalists to meet their families. She'd expressed how much she loved Sean's family and even said she could see herself moving with him to Dallas. But now in Curaçao they'd have a day just to themselves. They hopped onto a plane and flew to a small private island. They went snorkeling and had dinner on the beach. Sean talked about being a father to her daughter.

"At that point I was sure that I was going to win this show and I was going to marry her," he says. "We also had a common bond that she didn't share with the other two guys still left on the show. I'm a believer, and she's a believer. It wouldn't make sense with anybody else."

After Sean had his day with Emily, the other two contestants had their days with her. Sean spent those days dreaming about the future. He had no doubt that God had orchestrated this entire journey. He would soon be married and become a father. He hadn't planned on being on the show, meeting someone like Emily, or falling in love. But here he was just one episode away from a whole new life.

"I had no doubt in my mind whatsoever," he admits.

Audience members had watched the many other dates Emily had gone on and knew that Sean wasn't the only one she had feelings for. By week nine, all three of the remaining suitors had found a place in her heart. While Sean believed he'd already found his match, the rest of the world wasn't so sure, and neither was she.

At the end of each episode, the bachelorette is given roses to hand out to each man she wishes to see continue on the journey. In week nine she had two roses, but three men to choose from. Sean never got a rose.

"I couldn't understand," Sean confesses. "Why would she send me home when I thought she was falling in love with me? I was certainly in love with her. I went back to Dallas heartbroken. I had never had my heart broken, ever. I had always been the guy who had called it off with the girls I had dated. Heartbreak was a foreign concept for me. I poured my heart out for this girl, Emily. I was convinced that God had presented her to me to marry and be the father of her daughter. But then it ended in heartbreak. I didn't know what hit me."

Sean wondered what he could have done differently. Where had he gone wrong? Should he have said something that he didn't? Was it something he did? He even tried to call Emily to ask her these questions, but he never got a response.

"But even in my darkest hour," Sean says, "I knew that God had bigger plans for me. I knew that God was going to use that experience for something greater."

Behind the scenes of the show, Sean had continued to live out his faith. He'd shared a living space with more than a dozen other men, and many of them had noticed that he started his day by reading the Bible and a devotional to help keep his life focused on Jesus. He'd even been able to introduce Jesus to several of the men, who had never heard much more than the name. Looking back, Sean could see some purpose in those interactions. Perhaps they'd even been the reason God chose to put him on the show.

While he didn't fully understand what God had in mind, Sean trusted that he had a plan for his love life. Meanwhile he spent the following weeks catching up with the rest of America by watching the show he'd just costarred in. "Being able to watch that all unfold on TV and see her relationships with the other guys play out was therapeutic for me," he says. "It helped me get over her quicker."

Sean had signed up for the show with a plan in mind. As the weeks unfolded, he'd thought he could see another plan, God's plan, come into play. But now that both plans had left him surprised and heartbroken, he waited to see what God would have for him next. And that's when he got a call.

"It was about six weeks later that I got a phone call from one of the executive producers on *The Bachelor*," he says. Started in 2002, and now in its twenty-fifth season, *The Bachelor* was the flagship show that had spawned the one he'd just been booted from. And the show's producers apparently wanted to feature Sean as season seventeen's bachelor.

Sean asked for a week to think and pray about the offer. He had some concerns—the same ones he'd had the first time around, plus several more.

"The concept of *The Bachelor* is absolutely nuts," Sean says. "It's unnatural to date twenty-five women at one time. It felt wrong. I was pretty sure God had opened this door, but what if he hadn't? What if he didn't want me to do the show? What if I'd harm my testimony by dating and kissing multiple people on national television?"

Sean felt proud of the image he had built on *The Bachelorette*. He'd maintained his character and his dedication to God. He'd stayed true to his faith, and people had noticed. He worried about undoing what good reputation he had built for God and for those who follow God.

"What if being on *The Bachelor* is going to damage that?" he recalls worrying. "I've got thick skin. I can take a lot of things. But what if people look at me and they say, 'This is what's wrong with Christianity'? *The Bachelor* has a stigma. Guys go on there, get drunk. There's the fantasy suite. There's sex and nudity. I never thought it represented me."

He took counsel from several people close to him, particularly his parents.

"Just because the show doesn't have the greatest reputation," his father told him, "that doesn't mean people won't see Jesus through you."

That response shocked Sean.

"He's the godliest man I've ever come in contact with," Sean says of his father. "What he said carried a lot of weight with me."

"You don't have to go on there and preach or give a sermon," his father reminded him. "People are going to see Jesus through you whether you're talking about him or not. God has opened this door for you. You owe it to yourself to walk through it."

Sean still had concerns about stepping into another crazy reality television show. He feared staining people's view of God, and he feared more heartbreak. But with his father's advice ringing in his ears, he decided to take the risk.

"I was ready to take it on," he says. "But it was a scary proposition. I was still really skeptical that I would find love again. That sounds funny because I fell in love on *The Bachelorette*, but I did not think it was going to happen on *The Bachelor*. I just promised myself to stay open-minded. I thought it would at least be a fun journey, an exciting ride."

As the episodes from *The Bachelorette* aired, people with similar convictions had reached out to him. He'd been open with Emily about his faith, as he would be with any woman he dated. He wasn't trying to show off or be provocative, but simply shared who he was. He followed Jesus, and he would want anyone he went out with to know that.

"I talked about it a few times with Emily, and they aired it," he recalls. "I didn't think that people would really take notice of it. But I was overwhelmed by the number of people that came up to me and thanked me for the stance for Jesus I took."

Sean's parents raised him in the faith. He grew up going to church. As he got older, he noticed he viewed the world differently than many of his friends, who didn't understand his faith or the choices that faith led him to make. This difference was heightened when he played Division I football at Kansas State and found himself surrounded by a culture that expected sex.

"I was ridiculed for not having sex by my teammates and by my friends," he says. The surrounding pressures and the temptations eventually led him to lose this focus.

"It was six years of emptiness," he says, referring to his early adulthood. "I knew the truth, but I started having sex. I would pray occasionally, go to church. I would say the right words sometimes to people who asked me what I believed in. But I had chosen this path of destruction. I knew that it was not the life that I was supposed to be living. And eventually it got to a point where I knew I needed to take ownership of my faith. I couldn't rely on my parents' faith or the faith of anyone else."

He chose to reclaim the path he had started on. He decided

to begin each day with prayer and reading the Bible to maintain that focus. It was this focus that he carried with him into *The Bachelorette* and determined to keep while on *The Bachelor*.

The whirlwind began again. Sean flew out to Los Angeles to start the shooting. The first night, twenty-five women lined up to meet and impress him. One did a backflip. Another brought a football, and one talked about her favorite books. Each came with her best attempt to grab Sean's attention and affections. The following weeks brought helicopters, an amusement park, a new Guinness World Record for on-screen kissing, a rock-climbing trip, and more. Soon the crowd started to narrow, and there was one person Sean just couldn't get enough of: Catherine Giudici.

"I couldn't see myself saying good-bye to her ever," Sean says. "It was always extremely difficult to end any day with her or any date that we had."

Catherine hailed from Seattle, Washington, where she worked in advertising. She and Sean spent their first one-on-one date together in snowy Alberta, Canada. They both felt a connection, but they barely knew each other. Sean, in particular, still needed to know more about Catherine's faith.

"You don't really have a chance to have a lot of serious conversations," Sean says about the early weeks of the show. "Before I went on *The Bachelor*, I made a list of things I needed in a wife. At the top of that list is that she has to love Jesus. As the weeks went by, I started to dive into faith on those dates. They don't show a lot of this on TV, of course. Catherine didn't know Jesus the way that I did. She had been raised Catholic, but she didn't know Jesus as her personal Lord and Savior."

That wasn't the plan. And Sean had had a lot of that recently. It wasn't the plan to lose his business. It wasn't the plan to go into insurance. It wasn't the plan to have his heart broken on *The Bachelorette*. And it wasn't the plan to fall for a girl who wasn't in the same place as he was with God. But even though events weren't working out exactly the way he'd planned, he could still sense God's guiding hand in it all. He didn't yet know where he was being led—or rather who he was being led to—but he knew that Catherine was special.

"There was just something there that let me overlook it," he says of their different experiences with faith. "I think God knew where her life was heading."

He wasn't just looking for a faith partner. He was looking for a friend, someone to go through life with and enjoy all the experiences that life offers. He saw all this in Catherine. They fell in love.

In the end Sean chose Catherine and bent to his knee with a proposal.

"If I had stuck to my original plan, I wouldn't have proposed to her," he admits. "We would not have a relationship, and we certainly wouldn't be getting married."

In the months that followed, Catherine would commit her life to follow Jesus. Sean couldn't know this at the time he chose her, but he had learned to trust God for his future.

"God has given me this woman who completely loves and adores him and who loves me as well," he says. "She is my absolute best friend. Catherine and I are like two teenagers in love when we're around each other. She is the most devoted woman that I've ever come across."

If Sean had kept to his own plans, none of this would have been possible. His experience in reality television and with Catherine has given him a unique trust in God's plan for the future. He has often contemplated his favorite passage from the Bible, which reads:

Now listen, you who say, "Today or tomorrow we will go to this or that city. We will spend a year there. We will buy and sell and make money." You don't even know what will happen tomorrow. What is your life? It is a mist that appears for a little while. Then it disappears. Instead, you should say, "If it pleases the Lord, we will live and do this or that."[1]

"Why worry about today?" Sean asks. "Your eighty or ninety years on earth is just a blink of an eye compared to eternity. That really puts things in context. It doesn't matter what I go through, the ups or downs, because I've got a God who loves me. He's right there next to me saying, 'It's going to be okay. I've got plans for you. I love you.' What's more comforting than knowing that the Creator of the universe is also my best friend and that he's with me wherever I go?"

Not many people would choose to find love on reality television. Sean Lowe chose it twice. But each time he followed the winding, strange, but ever-so-sure path of God. He knows his God has wonderful plans in the future for him and for his now wife, Catherine. They married in January 2014 and have three children. He's learned that the God who was creative enough to invent the universe has plenty of creative juice left to make life interesting.

If you are still looking for your love or struggling with one you have, God has not forgotten you. Wherever you find yourself on your journey of love, you can trust that there is a loving and creative God with a plan for you too. It won't be the plan you invent, coerce, or imagine. It will be his plan. But his plans are sure, full of adventure, and better than anything you could hope for.

in search of
Belonging

Everyone needs a place where they feel normal.

Have you ever noticed that rebels all dress the same? People who shout out their rejection of culture don't leave culture behind. They just create their own. The hippie movement famously rejected cookie-cutter mainstream American life and chose unconventional lifestyles. Yet as a group they listened to similar music, ate similar food, started communes where similar-minded people could live together, and even developed their own distinctive style of dress that is still caricatured today. Whether it's pale skin and black eyeliner (goth), ragged flannel (grunge), baggie pants, tattoos, or backward hats, each outward display of rebellion also makes a declaration of belonging.

Humans are social creatures. It's in our nature. In addition to food, clothing, and a place to sleep, people need people. In the same breath that we say, "I am different . . ." we can't help but add, "just like these people." People insist they must be unique and special, but even in making that declaration we are all alike.

Normal is what we all want most. We may struggle to admit it. But the truth is we don't so much want to be different as we want others to think our differences are normal.

In the pages to come, you will find the stories of loners who found belonging. They felt lost, different, rejected, and isolated, but God declared them family. The farther they wandered in this world, the more God sought them for the next. In him the friendless found a Friend, the fatherless found a Father, and the incomplete found wholeness. Perhaps, as you read their stories, you will find that you are not alone in your aloneness.

You belong.

Chapter 6

Unworthy

limit of love

BETH NIMMO, MOTHER OF COLUMBINE VICTIM
TJ STEVENS, SCHOOL SHOOTER

There are limits to God's love.

Certainly, there must be.

Some people are too far gone. They have done too much.

At least that is what many people would be tempted to think if—like Beth Nimmo—their child were murdered at school.

On April 20, 1999, Beth's daughter, Rachel Scott, became the first of the thirteen victims killed in the Columbine High School massacre in Colorado.

Beth recalls how she first learned about the incident. "There's been a shooting at Columbine," she heard on the phone. Beth's oldest daughter had called her at work to tell her to turn on the television. Millions would watch the broadcast, though few with such anxiety as this mother of five. In addition to her daughter,

Beth also had a son, Craig, who attended the high school. She recalled them leaving for school that morning.

"Rachel shouted for Craig to hurry," Beth says. "He always made her late to school. She yelled out that she loved me and then ran out the door with Craig."

The shooting began at approximately 11:19 in the morning. The two shooters originally planned to bomb the cafeteria, which could have killed hundreds. But when the explosives failed to detonate, they entered the school, choosing to fire at their classmates. Within fifteen minutes of opening fire, twelve students and a teacher were dead, and another twenty people were wounded. The shooters would turn their guns on themselves shortly after noon.

Beth waited anxiously into the afternoon before she heard from her son.

"I'm okay," Craig said. "But I can't find Rachel."

Confusion ruled in the hours that followed the initial reports. Rumors were reported as fact. Terrorized and confused victims had their recollections retold to millions as reporters began crowding around the school. But nobody could tell Beth anything about her daughter Rachel.

"It's bad, Mom," Craig repeated over the same phone call. "It's really, really bad."

Craig had escaped unharmed from the school library, the bloodiest scene of the day, where ten of the day's murders had taken place. After a firefight with police, the shooters had ended their lives in that same room.

"As they secured the school, they were busing the kids to one of two places," Beth remembers. School officials attempted an evacuation of the remaining students. They posted lists of the students that were accounted for. Beth frantically checked the lists throughout the day but never found Rachel's name. Finally, as darkness descended on the scene, officials sent her home.

"If you haven't heard from a hospital or your child wasn't on a bus," she was told, "then we need you to fill out a missing-person report."

Beth obeyed, only to be told to return home with no additional information.

Nearly twenty-four hours after the shooting at Columbine began, Beth finally received confirmation of her daughter's death. Though the shooters had taken their lives shortly after noon the day before, police didn't clear the building for many hours afterward. Confusion continued to mire down official efforts. But finally someone told Beth and other parents like her the bad news.

"I remember sinking down to the floor," she says. "Nothing was real. Total disbelief. There were a lot of those days after that I just can't remember."

But as Beth's family mourned her loss, they also began discovering more about Rachel's faith.

"We started discovering writings and journals," Beth says. "She had a really deep relationship with the Lord. On the back of a dresser she had outlined her hands. In the middle of that outline she'd written a message: 'These are the hands of Rachel Joy Scott and will someday touch millions of people's lives.'"

"And Rachel was right," reflects her mother. "She just didn't know she was going to have to die to do it."

The more Rachel's family read in her journals and the more they talked with those who knew her, the more her faith and kindness shone brightly.

"God had put a great gift in our home. She was loved by all of us. We cherished her. But we had no idea what God's purpose for her life and her death was."

After her death, many of Rachel's classmates and friends reached out to Beth and shared with her the many acts of kindness they had received from her. She'd had an eye for those who were bullied or hurting. They even heard a story of how she helped to prevent one young person from taking his own life.

Realizing the effect that Rachel and her story had on people, Beth's family started an organization to tell her story and share her kindness. Rachel's Challenge[1] has now grown into one of the most popular school programs in the nation. Rachel's legacy of kindness inspired the organization to teach students to replace bullying and violence with contagious kindness. Since its founding, the organization's school programs have had an impact on more than twenty-five million students.

"I have this theory," Rachel had written in one of her last school essays, "that if one person can go out of their way to show compassion, then it will start a chain reaction of the same. People will never know how far a little kindness can go."

In the twenty-plus years since her daughter's death, Beth Nimmo has preached this message of contagious kindness. She is convinced that it is through kindness—not judgment or bitterness—that the cycle of violence can end. And it was in that same spirit that she agreed to sit down with TJ Stevens.

TJ never felt worthy of kindness—not after what he had done. After all, God could never forgive a school shooter, right?

It was nine o'clock in the morning on a fall day in 1982. Frances Churchman had just entered the office of her son's suburban Virginia high school to drop off clothes for him when she saw James Stevens (who now goes by the nickname TJ) with a rifle in his hands.[2]

"Oh, they're promoting *Oklahoma!*," she thought. She had seen the school musical the night before. She assumed TJ came dressed like a frontiersman from the play. He wore a sheepskin jacket and carried a high-powered Mossberg hunting rifle with a scope attached to the top.

"I want you over on that side!" the young man shouted. Nobody took him seriously. Neither Frances nor anyone else in the office moved. A slight chuckle rolled through the room at his theatrics.

"I mean business!" he insisted. He fired the gun into the light fixture above, and glass exploded across the floor. The laughter of a moment before transformed into screams.

"I just started shooting," TJ now remembers. "I shot down the hallway, but always above people's heads. Kids started running and screaming."

His girlfriend's words from the night before still rang in his ears.

"I can't see you anymore," she had told him. He wanted to marry her, but instead she'd ended the relationship. After this, the last in a string of disappointments, he'd decided to end his life.

"She was the one thing out of so many things that I'd lost," he recalls feeling. "I refused to lose her."

TJ's father had left the family when he was three. Then his stepfather had abused him and other members of the family. "I feared for my life," he says, referring to his abusive stepfather. "I feared for my mom's life and my brother's life."

He had translated the hate at home into a tough-guy appearance at school. He'd kept to himself, thinking of himself as the black sheep of the school. Frustrated and angry, he'd dropped out the year before, taking a job at a nearby clothing store. Now, with the loss of his girlfriend, he was convinced he had nothing left to live for.

He went into his room and turned off the lights. He bent down to his knees and picked up his gun. The barrel scraped against the roof of his mouth. His finger on the trigger, he began applying pressure.

But then he heard the voice—not an audible voice, but a voice in his head that felt like it came from outside of him.

"If you do it the way I'll show you," he heard it say in a cool, even tone, "then I'll give you the peace you're looking for."

Peace. That's what he wanted. Death would surely give him that. But with visions of violent revenge flooding his mind, he took the gun out of his mouth and looked at it with new eyes. He'd still end his life, but he would take others with him.

"They're going to pay," the voice continued, blending in with his own thoughts now. Revenge for all the perceived wrongs and slights would be his. He grabbed his hunting rifle and began counting out shells.

"I methodically counted each shell," he remembers, "putting names on the bullets."

If I kill this person or the other, it'll take away the pain, he thought.

As he shot down the hallway, scattering his former classmates, he recalled all those names.

After firing his weapon, he had moved from the hallway into the school office, where he held two school officials hostage, including school principal John Alwood. (He didn't know it yet, but eight other hostages were trapped in a nearby supply room, including Frances Churchman.) So started what would become a twenty-one-hour standoff between Stevens and the police, represented by chief negotiator Don Grant.

"If you don't do what I tell you to do," Stevens remembers threatening Don, "then I'm going to line bodies up in the hallways one by one with your name on them."

But something held him back from carrying out his threat, even when he discovered the hostages in the supply room and the voice in his head, the one from the night before, returned.

"You are a failure!" the voice accused.

"You are nothing!" he heard again.

The voice in his head multiplied to a chorus: "Kill these people now!"

But something else also battled within him, a presence deep inside his heart that restrained him.

"When I walked in that morning, I had no emotion," he remembers. "There was no trying to talk myself out of it. No tears were falling."

But as time wore on, this other presence won out against the rage and the pain. Gradually he came to realize the lie he had swallowed.

"Something was fighting me," he says. "It started fighting all the lies I had believed, the thoughts of revenge."

But Stevens feared that the voices calling for vengeance would overwhelm him. "Get out!" he growled to them in a low, inhuman voice. Then he stuck the barrel of the gun into his mouth once again.

"No more!" he told himself. "I'll kill myself so you can't kill these people."

Just then a woman to his right fell on her knees, facing him, pleading, "No! Don't do this!" She covered her face with her hands, rocking as she spoke. "You haven't killed anyone. You're just a kid. You don't need to do this."

A flash of light reflected off a cross she wore on her neck. As his captive pleaded, not for her life but for his, he saw shining on her a symbol of hope.

"The light pierced my eye as she rocked back and forth," he recalls.

A vision swept through his mind. He saw an arm reaching into the darkness and offering to lift him up. He reached back.[3]

"As soon as I did, my heart became human again," he says. "There were no more voices. Everything changed after that. Emotion overwhelmed me. I experienced pain, not only for everyone in the room but for their families too."

After holding his hostages for more than a dozen hours, TJ began releasing them one by one until the following morning when the last hostage walked out unharmed. He slid his gun out of the room on the floor and surrendered to police.[4]

TJ would later be sentenced to twenty years in prison.

Two years into his prison sentence, he chose to put Jesus first in his life.

"I have shown the world what I can do with my life," he prayed. "Now you take it and show the world what you can do with it."

He had entered that school looking for relief. The voice in his head had promised healing through vengeance and life through death. But Jesus had battled through the darkness and reached down to a lost soul. TJ saw the light moments before carrying his dark plans to completion. That was when he found the first taste of healing. When he gave his life to Jesus, that was a second taste.

While still in prison TJ was selected for a special program for people who had committed serious crimes but had not harmed anyone in the process. He went on to teach children with Down syndrome to play guitar as a part of the program. And because he successfully completed the program, his twenty-year sentence was reduced. Four and a half years after his arrest, he was a free man.[5]

TJ went on to rebuild his life the best he could. Over the next thirty years he married, had children, furthered his education, and built a career. He also wrote songs, sang in churches, and even played Jesus in Easter pageants. But he refused to speak to media or to share his story. His sense of shame over his crime only increased over the years.

"I don't feel worthy of this conversation," he told Beth Nimmo when they finally sat down to talk.

"You recognized the voice of truth," Beth reminded him. "You didn't know who that was then, but something in your heart caused you to reach for that hand that came toward you."

It has taken a while, but TJ is finally beginning to recognize that truth. And that's why, after decades of silence, he has chosen to make his story known. "My God, my God," he prays. "I never imagined in a thousand lifetimes that you were going to do this, that you would show the world what you can do with a high school shooter."

Through his story TJ offers unique insight into the heart and mind of a mass shooter. Few even survive the initial event, and fewer still evidence the kind of transformation TJ has. But his story also reveals important truths about the realities of good and evil.

Just as voices of light and darkness battled for TJ in that school, there are two kingdoms battling for dominance in this world. One, the kingdom of darkness, seeks to steal, kill, and destroy. It exchanges death for more death, pain for yet more pain. But the kingdom of light—God's kingdom—offers love without cost and without exception. No matter the depth of the sin or the darkness of a person's soul, God offers love, life, and forgiveness. For someone like TJ, forgiveness may be the most precious gift of all.

"Father, forgive them," Jesus famously prayed for those who tortured him on the cross.[6] In his dying breath he pleaded for the Father in heaven to forgive the very people who nailed him to a cross. In all the years since leaving prison and starting a new life, TJ has struggled to grasp the depth of this forgiveness.

"I don't want to waste what he's given me," he said to the Columbine mother. "You turned your pain into passion, and you're changing lives. My prayer is that I can do the same with the pain that I created."

In talking with Beth, TJ named the two words that have defined his life since giving his life to Jesus: *earn it*. But Beth urged him to "rethink those words. You don't have to earn anything. God doesn't expect things of us. Without him we can do nothing. Instead of 'earn it,' just walk in it. Walk in the gift."

"For it is by grace you have been saved, through faith—" she reminded him with a verse, "and this is not from yourselves, it is the gift of God—not by works."[7]

TJ is learning that there is a fine but important line between earning and reciprocating. It's the difference between cause and effect. To earn something means we bring about a deserved outcome. We earn a paycheck, a grade, or an award. But reciprocation is merely a response to something we had no part in bringing about. It's the effect that follows the cause. When we receive a gift, you reciprocate with a thank-you, a note, or a gift in return. But none of these actions caused the initial gift, nor do they make us more deserving of the gift. They are simply the proper response to an act of grace and kindness.

"I'm sorry for your pain," Beth said after hearing TJ tell his story. "I'm sorry for the events of your life that led you to feel so desperate, to take that kind of desperate action. But I rejoice in your redemption."

Beth and TJ come from opposite sides of the same kind of tragic event—a school shooting. But they both have come to understand the same truth: light overcomes the darkness. God can and does take the darkest evil and turns it into the brightest beacon of hope.

No matter what side of life's story you find yourself on, whether you're a victim or a victimizer (or both), God is on your side. And if God is for you, who can be against you? He is reaching through the darkness, extending his hand for you. You don't need to earn it. His love did all the earning for you.

Will you reach back?

NHL star Mike Fisher and his wife, Carrie Underwood, found themselves reaching out to God in a time of tremendous loss. They needed to know he could take their cries of pain. His response changed them forever.

Chapter 7

Valleys

wrestling
with loss

MIKE FISHER, FORMER NHL STAR
CARRIE UNDERWOOD, SINGER AND SONGWRITER

For most of Mike Fisher's life, success meant one thing: hockey.

"I always said I wanted to be an NHL hockey player," says Mike Fisher, who retired in 2018 after nineteen years in the National Hockey League. "I loved to compete. I loved the speed of it. I loved to score. People would ask me what I wanted to be when I grew up. It was an NHL hockey player every time. That's all I ever wanted to do."

Mike's Canadian hometown of Peterborough, Ontario, overflowed with kids like him who wanted to make it big in hockey. Ice rinks dot the landscape of the eighty-thousand-person city. The local minor-league team, the Peterborough Petes, is the oldest continuously operating team in the Ontario Hockey League and has produced more NHL players than any junior team in the world. And Mike just knew he was going to be part of that tradition.

"I can still remember feeling teachers or other students doubt me," he says. "But that was what I worked hard for. I was a determined little kid."

Mike was willing to do almost anything to reach his goal. He lived and breathed the dos and don'ts of becoming a star athlete. The trouble is, that "get it done" attitude bled into how he viewed his relationship with God.

"I grew up in a Christian family," Mike remembers. "My own story of faith begins at six years old. I was about to go to school. I asked my mom if I could ask the Lord into my heart. That was the beginning of a journey of ups and downs. At an early age I thought I needed to please him by doing right things and not doing wrong things. Hockey is a stats-related, a performance-based sport. That carried over into a more authoritarian view of God. I focused too much on trying to be a good kid."

By the age of seventeen, Mike Fisher was drafted into the Ontario Hockey League and, shortly after that, into the NHL. The Ottawa Senators selected him in the second round, forty-fourth overall, in the 1998 draft.

"I made my childhood dream," he remembers. "I made it to the NHL. I was making a great salary. Everything was great on the outside. But inside I was struggling."

For so long Mike had focused on doing what he thought God wanted rather than developing a real relationship with him. And he figured that so long as he did the right things, he'd be right with God. Be a good person—meaning don't swear, don't drink, don't have sex outside of marriage—and then God will like you.

But the trouble with such a rules-based theory of God is that it makes no allowance for temptation, failure, or mistakes—which all of us face at one time or another. That happened to Mike in his first few years of the NHL. "I started partying too much," he says, "trying to make impressions and making friends in the wrong way."

As the youngest player on the team, he felt a pressure to fit in with his older peers. But when he gave in to that pressure, the dream that was supposed to give him happiness turned into a source of frustration and ever-increasing guilt. "I knew what was right, but I wasn't doing it," Mike recalls.

"That was the worst time in my life," he says, "when it should have been the best. I was letting people down. I was letting God down."

Mike's relationship with God had always been stuck in the just-do-the-right-thing gear and had never made it to a place of deeper love and trust. So when he found himself doing the wrong thing, he couldn't figure out how to make things right with God.

"I still went to church," he says of those early years, "but maybe I'd be hungover. I tried to pretend like everything was great. But that's when I started doing a Bible study with my cousin"—a study that would completely change his thinking about God and about his life.

One day the two of them talked through a passage in the

gospel of Mark: "If any of you wants to be my follower, you must give up your own way, take up your cross, and follow me."[1]

Those words of Jesus hit Mike hard because they contrasted so sharply with the way Mike was living. He had spent all his energies from an early age in pursuit of one thing: hockey. He'd focused mind, body, and spirit on working toward that success. But success in hockey didn't lead to him feeling successful with God.

Mike realized that God was disappointed in many of the temptations he'd fallen into. But he also realized that God wanted more than obedience to a set of rules.

What God wanted was Mike's heart—that part of his life that he'd always held back.

"If you give up your life for my sake . . ." the passage continues, "you will save it. And what do you benefit if you gain the whole world but lose your own soul?"[2]

"That scripture was for me," Mike says. "I had reached my dreams. I had money. But my life just wasn't working, and I knew why. I hadn't been looking for life in the right places."

From then on, Mike began to change. It didn't happen in a day, a week, or a month. But gradually, over time, God began to reshape Mike's heart.

"God became real to me," he remembers. "He changed me on the inside. I started to not worry so much about the dos and don'ts and focused instead on pursuing him. It wasn't religion anymore. It was a real relationship. It was awesome."

Mike would learn to rely on this growing relationship with God when he and Carrie Underwood faced the most difficult challenge of their marriage.

Carrie Underwood first rose to fame as a contestant on season four of *American Idol*. She hailed from rural Checotah, Oklahoma, and brought to the show a powerful voice and stories of feeding hay to the animals on her family's farm. She'd grown up singing at local talent shows, community events, and the First Free Will Baptist Church. But by the time she began attending university, she had left behind any serious hope of building a music career. *American Idol* was to be final confirmation that it was time for her to move on.

She'd go on to dominate the season, ultimately winning the season, and become the show's most commercially successful artist. She has since sold more than sixty-five million records worldwide and has won countless prestigious awards, including seven Grammy Awards. But if her musical success surprised this small-town girl, so has marriage and motherhood.

"I feel like it has exceeded all of my expectations," she says. "I never thought about getting married or having a family. I don't know why. There's no reason for it. I have great parents and siblings. But I've always done very well by myself. So having my own family has been a pleasant surprise."

Mike Fisher and Carrie Underwood met in late 2008, with the help of a friend. They soon began dating and were married by the summer of 2010. But they spent the early part of their marriage living in different countries—she in Nashville, Tennessee, and he in Ottawa, Canada, playing for the Ottawa Senators.

Mike and Carrie had faith in common. They had both grown

up following Jesus. But events in their marriage and family would soon push them into unknown territory.

"It sounds wrong when you say it, but it's one of those bad things that happens to other people," Carrie remembers feeling. "It's not something you ever envision yourself having to deal with."

It all began when they decided to have a second child.

The couple had announced the birth of their son, Isaiah Michael, in 2015. But then, as Mike puts it, "We wanted him to have a little brother or sister."

"I am a planner," Carrie adds. "I like to know what's happening all the time. So we started planning, and we got pregnant again."

Just a couple of months into the pregnancy, they lost the baby.

They prayed and tried again.

They miscarried again.

"After the second miscarriage, I was frustrated," Mike remembers.

Then came a day when he spoke to God with raw honesty. It all came out—the pent-up frustration and anger, the confusion about why God would allow this to happen.

"I was wrestling with God," Mike remembers. "I was the most honest I'd been with him ever in my life."

And in that moment God answered him clearly.

"I heard him, not audibly, but I could sense God telling me that we were going to have a son and his name would be Jacob."

The name of the man who famously wrestled with God in the Bible,[3] *Jacob* became a promise in Mike's mind. He was convinced that God would give them another child.

But when Carrie miscarried a third time, Mike began to question. "Was I hearing things right?" he wondered.

Carrie was questioning too. "Where is God?" she remembers asking during that time.

The next day, after Mike left to go fishing, Carrie went up to where Isaiah was sleeping. She crawled into bed with him and had a really honest conversation with God.

"Isaiah is such a happy, loving, wonderful child," she explains. "I never wanted to complain. I never wanted to seem ungrateful. But I told God how hurt I felt. You feel guilty for being mad at your Creator. But I was angry. I needed to either have a baby or not, ever. I couldn't keep going down this road anymore."

In any relationship there are defining moments, points in time that reshape everything that follows. Mike and Carrie both had now crossed one of those points with God. They loved God. They trusted him. But they also felt anger and frustration. It was the end of the honeymoon phase and the start of something deep and multidimensional.

"I will forever feel like I had that moment with God," Carrie remembers. "I told him how I felt, and I told him I needed something. I feel he heard me."

"That was the only time in our lives where I think we really wrestled with God," Mike says. "We weren't demanding that he give us his blessing, the way Jacob did in the Bible. But we were being honest with him."

Then, after three miscarriages in just over a year, Carrie became pregnant again. Jacob Bryan Fisher was born healthy on January 21, 2019. God is good

There was a man in the Bible whose job it was to bring terrible news from God to a people who had lost touch with him. Their prayers had become empty and hollow. They went through religious motions, but never emotions. They loved the scent and feel of faith rituals but had no real desire for their Creator's presence. In fact, they kept worshiping false gods.

So God determined to bring his people back to him, no matter what it took. Granting them blessings had failed, but surely they would listen to calamity. So God told them, through Jeremiah, that famine would come and foreigners would invade the land, taking his people into captivity.

But even in sending this hardship, God was still only shouting his love. "I know the plans I have for you," he told them through Jeremiah, "plans to prosper you and not to harm you, plans to give you hope and a future. . . . You will seek me and find me when you seek me with all your heart. I will be found by you . . . and will bring you back from captivity. I will gather you from the . . . places where I have banished you."[4]

"It's so true," Mike says after quoting the same verse. "We've had all these mountaintop experiences in life. I always wanted to play hockey, and that's what I was able to do. Carrie always wanted to sing, and that's what she was able to do. But this was the first real valley we went through together. God was asking us, 'Do you trust my will?'"

It was exactly when Mike and Carrie felt most abandoned by God that he leaned in closest to them.

"When you go through the valleys, you really seek him," Mike says. "That's when you learn and grow. He changes you. We don't understand everything, and we never will. There's going to be more heartbreak in our lives. We know it's coming. But I know God is inherently good.

"I realized my goal of playing in the NHL when I was nineteen, and that was probably the emptiest I'd been as a person. It should have been the best, but it wasn't. That was because I wasn't living for God. Apart from a real relationship with God there is no true happiness."

"There are bad things that happen in the world," Carrie adds. "But through it all I want the people in my life to know that they are loved by God, that they are wanted. I feel like that's my job, if I could just make everybody feel that they are loved. God has real unconditional love for his children."

It's often in the hard spots of life that we can best hear the love of God. Perhaps that's why he lets those times come. He's been shouting his unconditional and unearnable love since the day he created you and me. But we don't always hear him until things go wrong and we desperately need him. Then suddenly there he is, exactly where he has always been.

In a similar way, Chad Robichaux also found love and belonging through hardship. But his journey to belonging brought him to the middle of a war zone in Afghanistan—and later a near deadly battle with PTSD.

Chapter 8

Aftermath

post PTSD

CHAD ROBICHAUX, MARINE AND MMA FIGHTER

"My father joined the military to end his life," Chad Robichaux says. During the height of the Vietnam War, Chad's father crashed his car into a garbage truck on the way to school. His friend, who was riding with him, died in the accident. Racked with guilt, he decided to end his life by signing up as an infantryman in the middle of the bloody war. But when he didn't die, he returned home a damaged man.

"They didn't have things in place at that time to really help or support veterans coming home," Chad explains.

The terms used to describe war-related mental and emotional trauma have differed across the ages. But even the ancients recognized that soldiers often return home with wounds that cannot be seen. From Herodotus to Hippocrates and all the way through the modern era, writers and historians have described the nightmares, emotional instability, or tendency toward violent and reckless behavior as the sad consequence of these hidden wounds. It's been called soldier's heart, shell shock, combat fatigue, and, in the Vietnam era, gross stress reaction.

But it wasn't until many years after Vietnam that psychologists recognized the long-term nature of the mental and emotional trauma that veterans face. They gave it the name *post-traumatic stress disorder* (PTSD). The common belief up to that time was that wartime trauma was short-term in its effects. This disqualified veterans from any long-term care, leaving men like Chad's father without the support they needed.

"He became a drunk, an abuser, and a womanizer," Chad recalls. "From very early on, my childhood was surrounded by this chaos. I really didn't have the father figure that I desired my whole life."

Chad's father abused both Chad and his mother. After he abandoned the family, Chad's stepfather ended up doing the same.

"Anyone that's really grown up in a dysfunctional home like that knows that siblings get really close," Chad says. He and his brother, who was just a year older, bonded through the violent outbursts of their dysfunctional family. But then, at the age of fifteen, Chad's brother was shot and killed. His tragic death sent Chad's mother into a severe depression. When his stepfather grew tired of her struggle to cope, he, too, left the family. With his father absent, his stepfather gone, his mother mired in depression, and his brother dead, Chad found himself alone.

"I had just given my life to God earlier that year, after a friend invited me to church," Chad remembers. "But I didn't understand how God could allow this to happen to my brother at such a young age. I became very angry and very isolated. I removed myself from a relationship with anyone."

Chad drifted away from God in the aftermath of his brother's death. He struggled to trust in a loving God who could allow such pain and tragedy, and eventually he gave up trying. His attitude would reveal itself in the description embossed on the military identification tags he would wear around his neck as a marine. Commonly called dog tags, these metal identifiers list basic information related to a soldier, including religious affiliation.

"I recently found my dog tags from when I went to boot camp," Chad says. "I had imprinted on my tags 'none' for religious preference. Seeing that now reminds me of how hopeless and alone I felt in my life at the time. I was so desperate for a fresh start, something new."

Chad's father had served in the US Marine Corps, and though Chad hadn't had a relationship with him, he found some type of connection in joining him on that path.

"Him being a marine inspired me to want to do that," he says. "I began to train and prepare myself to be in the Marine Corps and to go into some type of special operations."

Typically, new recruits are required to have a high school diploma or its equivalent. But when Chad shared his family story with Staff Sergeant Brown at the local recruiting office, he was granted an exception.

"He had a heart for my situation," Chad recalls. "They ended up enlisting me at just seventeen years old without a high school diploma. I grabbed hold of that because for me it was a second chance at life."

Feeling isolated and fatherless, Chad found that the marines filled a hole in his life.

"It offered me the chance to learn how to be a man when my father wasn't able to teach me," he says. "I felt that God had abandoned me. My father had left me. So I just dove into the program. I ended up finding a great deal of success."

In his first year, Chad tried out for and was accepted into the Marine Corps' Force Reconnaissance, a special operations asset. Force Recon is challenged with operating independently behind enemy lines, performing tasks that are uniquely dangerous and difficult. It is the marine version of the Navy SEALs or the Army Green Berets, and it is considered one of the most elite fighting forces ever to walk on the planet.

But for Chad, there was little actual fighting to be done. This was before America's ongoing conflicts in Iraq and Afghanistan. "Without anything going on in the world, we trained all the time," he recalls.

During this time he met Kathy. They began dating and soon married at the young ages of eighteen and nineteen. They made the choice to start a family and switch from active duty to reserves. So Chad looked for a civilian job.

"We decided the best thing for me to do was to be a police officer," he remembers. "We thought it would give me some job experience."

Chad joined the St. Charles Parish Sheriff's Department just west of New Orleans as a deputy. But in his first year on the force, he faced a situation that few officers see in a lifetime of service.

It began as a domestic violence call. A fellow deputy put out on the radio that he needed backup. His voice sounded uncharacteristically panicked.

Chad rushed to the scene to find the deputy and a woman arguing on the porch. She wouldn't leave the entrance to her home. Her husband had barricaded himself into a back room with a gun. The officers needed her to retreat to a safe distance.

"But she wouldn't go," Chad says. "Eventually I ended up having to physically push her away from the porch."

The woman and her children were now outside in the crowd. Her husband was still inside, armed with a rifle.

"Let's talk about this," Chad shouted in. Standing in the doorway to the living room, he could look into a mirror and see the man around the corner. Chad warned him to leave the gun behind, and he seemed to be responding.

"He was yelling at me that he was coming out," Chad remembers. "Then he turned the corner, and he faced me."

The man held the rifle over his shoulder, testing the young officer's resolve.

"Legally I could have shot him right then," Chad recalls.

"I started yelling at the man to put down his gun or I would have to kill him," Chad says. The man refused. His wife could be heard screaming from the outside, making the situation more tense.

"I attempted to save him," Chad recalls. He jumped forward and put his hand on the rifle barrel, pushing it back. A brawl broke out.

"I kicked him and tried to get the gun away from him," Chad remembers. But the man was double Chad's weight and stood

nearly a foot taller. Even with Chad's Marine Corps training, sub-
duing a man of that size proved difficult.

"We were fighting with two guns. I realized at that point that
I had to save myself and my partner. So I shot him."

His partner followed suit. The man fell to his knees and
looked at Chad. In a plain, even tone he said, "You killed me."
Then he fell over and died.

"I had blood everywhere on me," Chad says. "I remember
trying to wash it off. I felt like I couldn't get it off of me. I could
hear his wife screaming and screaming."

Late that evening Chad returned home to Kathy, who had no
idea what he had just participated in and had gone to bed. "No
one had called her," Chad says. "I wanted someone to comfort
me because I had just killed this guy in front of his family. It was
something I never thought I would have a hard time with. I woke
her up to tell her what happened."

The next morning's newspaper came out with the headline
"Cold Blooded Murder," in reference to the killing. Shortly afterward Chad was indicted for second-degree murder, the risk of
jail time compounding the stress of the event. Though the grand
jury eventually cleared him of all charges and St. Charles Parish
granted him the Medal of Valor for his handling of the situation,
being accused still left him embittered.

Chad felt ever more isolated. His wife couldn't understand
what he was dealing with. The department hadn't supported him
over the course of the hearings. Though they did end up giving
him the award, it felt too little, too late. He thought back to his
time in the Marine Corps with new longing.

An opportunity to return to active duty came with the terrorist attacks of 9/11. "I got a phone call," Chad remembers. "They told me somebody had flown a plane into the World Trade Center. I knew at that moment it was a chance to go."

Within two weeks Chad had resigned his position as a deputy and later deployed to Afghanistan. This was where he found his sense of belonging, his brotherhood.

"It was the only brotherhood that I really had," he remembers feeling. "I wanted to be in Afghanistan all the time. I didn't even want to be home. At home my wife would worry about things that seemed trivial to me, like the kids needing to be at a sporting event. That's the most important thing in your world right now?

"She would pick me up from the airport after a deployment. Before we even got home, I wanted to be back in Afghanistan. I remember staring out the window looking at people doing things that seemed so irrelevant to me at that time. It made me angry and bitter toward my wife. But I didn't feel like I could tell her because I felt like she would reject it or not care. So I kept it to myself."

Many of the habits Chad had learned growing up in a broken home returned to him during this time. He isolated himself. He kept his feelings and his struggles secret. He built a wall between himself and his family and poured all his energies into his job as a soldier.

"I felt a personal obligation to my job and an obsession with it," he says. He felt a bond with his fellow marines. But being in a war zone took its toll on him.

"It's really hard to put into words," he says. "You see what a man can do to another man, what hatred can do. You can't make sense of it. You can't process it. And it wears on you. You've gone there to do something noble, but somehow you become what you came to fight—a person filled with hate."

Chad recalls a time he saw a man holding a young boy. Chad and a fellow soldier were driving. They weren't on any specific mission. This man ran up to their window, begging for help. In his arms was his grandchild, bloody and dying. He asked for money to get the boy to a hospital. Chad rolled down the window and gave him a single dollar bill.

"We could have helped him," Chad says. "We had nowhere to be. We had the time. What if that had been me with my child, needing to get him help? At what point had I become so cold that all I did was give him a dollar? I feel like I lost something of myself in Afghanistan. If I had seen something like that years before, my heart would have been broken."

Chad had told Kathy many times how cold and godless the war zone felt. In that moment he realized that he had let the coldness into his own heart. He had lost empathy for human life and compassion for his fellow man.

That coldness followed him around wherever he went, in the field or at home. "I remember going home, and my wife would be crying," he says. "I was telling her mean things and breaking her heart. I would think to myself, *Why don't I feel bad that I'm making my wife cry?* I wondered what was wrong with me as a husband that I didn't feel bad about that."

The same sense of numb coldness carried over into his relationship with his daughter. While home from another deployment, she had a birthday party. She complained about the color of the icing on her cake.

"I just took my hand and grabbed a handful of cake," he says. "I threw it against the wall and destroyed my daughter's birthday party. I was out of control, and I didn't feel bad about it. I can't explain in a way that makes sense that I felt bad for not feeling bad. But that's where I was with the people closest to me. I broke their hearts."

Though Chad had witnessed the fallout of his own father's PTSD, he failed to see the signs of the disorder in his own life. Emotional numbness is one of the most common symptoms, It functions as a defense mechanism. When extremely traumatic events occur, a person can become so overwhelmed that their emotions shut down entirely. Both negative feelings and positive ones are blocked. Interacting with loved ones becomes increasingly difficult without the usual emotional feedback. The result is the kind of emotional coldness and the kind of cruel acts he was beginning to display.

"I didn't know how to stop it," he says, remembering the increasing sense of hopelessness. "I felt like I shouldn't be in their lives anymore. They deserved a better husband and a better father. I felt disqualified."

The feelings of inadequacy sent Chad ever deeper into his role as a warrior. He signed up for a total of eight deployments. He saw a lot of death and evil. But what really ate at his mind was the loss of innocent life.

"Being personally involved with the loss of innocent life, for people working for me, that's where the trauma really crept in," he explains. "There were a handful of people who worked directly for me that I manipulated into a situation where they were captured and killed. It was hard reconciling that these people had trusted me. I felt responsible."

Chad still kept to himself the growing uneasiness and stress of his work as a marine. He feared people thinking of him as weak and unmasculine. Though he'd grown up knowing that his father had come back with postwar trauma, he still didn't have the vocabulary to describe his own struggles.

"I don't even know if we heard the words *post-traumatic stress disorder* before. It definitely wasn't something we talked about in our office. But I started to feel more and more of those symptoms. I began having physical numbness."

The emotional fallout of PTSD can manifest in physical ways, and this was happening to Chad. His arms and face would go numb without explanation. At first, he thought it was an allergic reaction or some other kind of ailment. Mental trauma was not something he knew to consider. As the symptoms increased in frequency and strength, he still feared talking about it with his fellow marines. Finally he shared it with his wife.

"I didn't tell her what was bringing on the stress, but I told her about the numbness," he says. "She was scared."

As another deployment approached, Chad felt a fear and an anxiety that he had long pushed away. "I remember it felt like my throat was swelling shut," he says. "I realized that I was having a panic attack. I had researched on the internet enough to know that. I went on deployment, got on the plane, and then couldn't get back off." When the plane landed at his destination and he attempted to stand, Chad felt his legs give out, and his whole body lost feeling.

"I can only remember bits and pieces of it," he says of that deployment. "I pretty much had it blacked out. I pushed my body so hard that my mind just zoned out."

When his panic attacks grew to blot out weeks' worth of memory, Chad knew he needed to get help. "I told my supervisors and my doctor what was going on when I came home from deployment, but only to a limited extent," he says. "I felt like I was losing my mind. I was afraid that if I told them exactly how I was feeling, they would put me in a straitjacket in a psych ward. I was in a constant state of panic, and my body would stop working at any moment. I would put myself in a panic attack in fear of the symptoms of a panic attack. I couldn't even be alone; I would start hyperventilating. My wife would try to hold me. She was extremely scared."

Chad's doctor diagnosed him with severe PTSD. A sense of failure came over him after the diagnosis. His supervisors had spoken of him as the golden boy of his Force Recon unit, and now he wasn't even allowed to deploy again. He'd gone in an instant from star quarterback to benched.

As the panic attacks worsened, Chad grew paranoid and terrified. This time at home wasn't like before. Before, he had been all anger and rage, and his family had walked on eggshells. But now he was quiet and scared, shaking—a broken person. Counseling gave him some relief, but he needed more.

"My wife and counselor brought up doing Brazilian jiu-jitsu," he says. This form of martial arts combines influences from various Japanese forms of fighting. It is known particularly for enabling fighters to force an opponent to submit through grappling, joint locks, and chokeholds.

Chad had studied martial arts as a part of his military training, but also as a hobby while on leave between deployments. He had even fought successfully in a number of professional bouts. But the focused approach of Brazilian jiu-jitsu promised a new way of reorienting his mind. Rather than brute power, the techniques in this school focus on leveraging the strength of an opponent against him. The unique emphasis on strategic foresight would give Chad a way to move his attention away from his anxieties.

"When I got on those mats for the first time, I felt like I had found the cure for PTSD," he says. "I had to think about what was next. I had to pay attention to what I was doing. I couldn't think about Afghanistan, or somebody would choke me."

Turning his hobby of martial arts into a full-time focus gave Chad relief from many of the symptoms he struggled with. He found a new obsession and immediate success. He entered professional fights and went undefeated in all his early bouts. He rose to be ranked first in the world in his class. He opened a school, and students flocked to replicate his prowess on the mats.

But while the symptoms subsided, he never actually dealt with the PTSD.

"I never dealt with my anger," he says. "I never dealt with the questions I had with God. It all looked successful on the surface, but underneath was a destroyed family and a failing marriage. I still struggled to deal with panic attacks and to process the shame I felt from not finishing my job in Afghanistan. I felt hollow inside."

Instead of facing his problems, Chad only shifted them from overseas to on the mat. His newfound acclaim in the growing sport of mixed martial arts (MMA) gave him a steady crowd of fans but not the real relationships and counsel he needed.

"People would tell me what I wanted to hear. I wasn't healthy in my life, but nobody would tell me the hard things I *needed* to hear."

"I'd say the loneliest place I've ever been in was lying in bed with my wife's back turned toward me," he says. "I resented her for not cheering me on like everyone else did in the gym. So I started going outside of my marriage for the attention of other women, eventually walking into an affair."

Finally, Chad and Kathy separated. They sold their home and signed leases for separate places. They encouraged their children, rationalizing that the separation would be better for them because they wouldn't be around all the fighting and the arguing. The children didn't agree; they begged their parents not to separate. But Chad and Kathy ignored their pleas and moved apart.

It was that time alone that shook reality back into Chad's eyes. "It gave me an opportunity to look at my situation," he says. "I saw the destruction that I had brought on my wife and my children. I realized that my dad wasn't the problem. My brother dying wasn't the problem. God wasn't the problem. The sheriff's department, the military, Afghanistan, and the Taliban were not the problem. My wife wasn't the problem. I was the problem."

He had spent his whole life pinning his problems on everyone but himself. There was always another cause and another person to blame for his own actions. The realization brought an even greater sense of shame. He had failed at the most important aspect of his life: family. He'd spent eight deployments protecting those he loved from evil, only to destroy his own family in the process.

He could see only one solution. He picked up his gun, intending to end his life. He would permanently separate himself from the people he had hurt. He figured his death would protect them from the damage and the pain he'd caused and would likely cause in the future.

"I tried to talk myself into taking my life," Chad says. "I was so angry at God for letting things get to this point. But God kept me from pulling the trigger."

He thought of his children. "My kids follow everything I do. I just didn't want to leave that legacy for my children."

Meanwhile Kathy reacted the opposite way to their separation: she ran toward God. At that point she wasn't hoping for their marriage to be fixed. Chad had left, and he was openly with other women. But she still feared for his well-being. She pleaded for God to transform her husband to the man she'd known when they met. She prayed for the father of her children and for the man she once loved. Then she asked Chad a question that would end up saving his life.

"You had the discipline to become a Force Recon marine and serve on eight deployments," she said to him. "You disciplined yourself to be a top-ranked MMA fighter. How could you do all these things but quit when it comes to your family?"

The question shook Chad to the core. He realized he had disciplined himself for everything but the things that mattered most.

"I'd quit on my faith in God, on my role as a husband, on my role as a father, and even on my health," he realized. "I'd sworn to be this person for my country, a warrior to fight for people who couldn't defend themselves. But I had given up on all the things that mattered most."

He left that conversation with a radical decision. If he could bend his will to take down the world's greatest foes, he would do the same to defeat the destruction he'd let loose on his family.

He approached the task the way he would any mission. He took out pen and paper and listed the challenges that stood in front of him. He named the issues he'd need to confront and the emotional, relational, and mental training he'd need to undertake.

But every athlete needs a trainer. He looked at the people he'd surrounded himself with and knew that none of them could help him on this new path. They could teach him to shoot, grapple, and cut weight before a fight, but not how to be a father and husband. He had no one who could help him overcome his hardship from Afghanistan.

Kathy introduced him to a minister she knew from church, Steve Toth, and Chad went to see him as a possible mentor.

"It's not going to work," Steve said when he saw the plan Chad had written up. "You're going to fall on your face again."

"What?" Chad responded. "Why isn't it going to work?"

"You didn't put God in this plan."

As a soldier commits to obey a commander and a martial artist submits to his master, Chad decided to do the same for his new journey to be a better father and husband.

"I submitted my life to Christ," he says. "I allowed this mentor to walk me into a true relationship with God like I had never had before. All the pills I had taken, the counseling, the psychologists, and the programs I had done—none of it worked. But Steve walked me through a yearlong biblical mentorship process, and that made all the difference. I learned what it meant to be a man. It was the very same thing I'd gone to the Marine Corps for. I didn't get it from my father, but I found it through the Scriptures."

One of the passages that struck Chad particularly strongly tells the story of a people who had turned cold toward their God. Cruelty grew in the people's hearts. God called out to them again and again, but they gave no response and felt no compassion for the pain they caused. They abused the poor, mocked the widows, and enslaved the weak. Against all warnings, the people returned evil for good at every turn.

After many years of grace, God called down destruction on these people. But he also made a promise to all of them who would listen. "I will give you a new heart and put a new spirit in you," he promised. "I will remove from you your heart of stone and give you a heart of flesh."[1]

Something in that verse spoke to Chad. He recognized that his own heart had long ago gone to stone, and he wondered if God's promise could ever apply to him.

Meanwhile, he was struggling to win back his wife. Having suffered for many years under his indifference, anger, and cheating, she was understandably angry. She threw back at him all his failures and misdeeds and recalled all the ways he had abandoned her. But he kept pushing forward the way a warrior fights his foe or an athlete grapples with an opponent.

At that point it wasn't love that moved him—he couldn't feel love—but raw discipline. "I prayed that God would let me feel again," he says. "I still had that coldness and callousness. But I wanted to have compassion for Kathy and understand how she felt."

It was in the midst of one of these prayers that Chad actually felt his heart of stone turn to flesh. "I was overwhelmed with emotion," he says of the moment. "I cried for probably two hours. I was processing everything I had done, and I finally understood that promise from God."

For the first time, Chad tasted freedom from his PTSD. And bit by bit, as he surrendered more and more of his life to Jesus and to the truths of the Bible, Chad found healing. As his heart softened, he built trust with Kathy, and their marriage took new shape.

"It has been the most rewarding and amazing journey," he says. "When no pill, no counselor, nothing else worked, simply aligning my life with God worked. We've committed our lives to share this with other people."

After a lifelong struggle to truly belong, Chad found that giving his life to Jesus rebuilt love in his life. He didn't need to isolate or separate himself. He found true belonging through following Jesus. Aligning his life with God's design reshaped his marriage, his family, and his heart.

"I was born into adversity," he says. "I came from hardship and battled my way into adulthood. I fought in Afghanistan and in a cage. But it wasn't until I aligned my life with God that I learned to fight for what mattered most."

Chad and Kathy have brought that same fighting spirit to help others through their foundation, Mighty Oaks.[2] They offer intensive peer-based programs helping veterans and their families overcome PTSD, strengthen marriages, and identify their true purpose in life.

Chad and Kathy have learned to fight for their family—together. It's something the Ketterer family would have to learn as well. But with the added challenge of adopting children from troubled backgrounds. Through it all, they'd discover what it really means for God to adopt us into his family.

Chapter 9

Adopted

what love can do

MICHAEL KETTERER, SINGER

Michael Ketterer stepped out onto the stage hoping to move the audience as much with his story as with his song. This round of *America's Got Talent* auditions would be taped, edited, and later aired to more than twelve million viewers across the country.

Unlike many other shows of a similar format that focus on musical talent, *America's Got Talent* welcomes a broad array of acts, including dance, magic, acrobatics, and even stand-up comedy. Performers here hope to hear the almighty "golden buzzer" that skips them directly to the quarterfinals and marks them as a favorite to win.

But Michael wasn't focused on winning that night. Just walking out onto the stage would meet all his expectations. Behind him stood his wife, Ivey, and their six children, five of whom had been adopted through the foster-care system. And this moment was all about them.

All Michael's adopted children came from troubled backgrounds. Neglected and abused, they had struggled to survive. And "when you're surviving, you can't dream," Michael explains. "A child's thinking in such circumstances gets stuck on finding a place to sleep, a meal to eat, or other basic needs."

Michael had journeyed to the *America's Got Talent* stage to show his children they could go beyond those circumstances and learn to dream again.

After all, they wouldn't even be together if it hadn't been for dreams. When Michael and Ivey first got together, they dreamed of raising a large family. They married young, and Ivey got pregnant just two years after the wedding. Partway through the pregnancy, however, complications emerged. Ivey grew ill and was later diagnosed with preeclampsia. Characterized by high blood pressure and with the potential for major organ damage and even death, the condition is extremely serious. For Ivey it resulted in the premature birth of their daughter Sophia.

"We were sitting at Cracker Barrel," Michael remembers. "My wife started seeing flashes in front of her eyes. Her elbows had become so swollen that she couldn't even bend them. Not knowing what to do, I called my mother and asked her advice."

"Michael, I don't want to alarm you," she said, "but you need to get to the emergency room right now."

They rushed Ivey to the hospital. Within forty-five minutes of arriving, the doctors had performed a cesarean-section delivery of their new child. But the danger wasn't over. "Your wife has a 30 percent chance of making it through the night," the doctors warned him. "And your daughter has maybe a 10 percent chance of making it."

That night, Ivey suffered through multiple organ failure. A doctor told Michael to prepare for the worst. But Michael wasn't ready to do that. "My wife will live and not die," he asserted.

The doctor rolled her eyes and walked out of the room. The seasoned medical professional looked at this young man with optimism dripping from his words and figured reality would dry out his bold prediction soon enough.

But Michael's prediction came true. Miraculously, both Ivey and Sophia survived their ordeal. Though their road to recovery was long, both eventually returned to full health. But the doctors warned Ivey against ever getting pregnant again. If she did, she would risk much graver consequences. So Michael and Ivey made the choice at that young age to not have any more kids.

Despite the change of plans, the two of them both refer to the years that followed as "phenomenal" and "amazing." They loved being together and parenting their daughter. Then something strange began happening with Sophia.

"Our eight-year-old daughter began having dreams," Michael recalls. "They were repetitive dreams that came over the course of two years. In them there were always three little boys, who she knew as her brothers. And the youngest of the boys was always in danger."

Whenever Sophia would have these dreams and sense the danger, she would wake up and run to her father.

"Sophie, it's just a nightmare," he would say.

"No, Dad," she would say with tears in her eyes. "They are my brothers." Then she would insist that her parents find these lost brothers and adopt them.

Michael and Ivey were actually not opposed to the idea of adopting more children—though not three at once—but they assumed they couldn't afford it. "Even when our hearts started warming up to the idea of adoption, we had only ever heard about international or agency-based adoption. Either way, it was so much money."

Depending on the circumstances, the typical adoption through these routes costs between $20,000 and $45,000.[1] For a family like the Ketterers, who struggled financially, the price point made this otherwise appealing idea unattainable.

"Then we ran into a family that had adopted out of foster care," Michael says. And that chance meeting changed their lives.

Though caring for needy children has long been an unofficial part of American society, the nation had no organized approach to such care until 1853, when Charles Brace, a New York minister, established Children's Aid Society. That organization became the basis of the country's modern foster-care system.

Today nearly half a million children are in foster care after being removed from their immediate families due to issues like neglect and abuse.[2] This intermediate step before adoption allows courts to determine whether the children will ever be able to return to their birth families. When they are not, foster families may choose to adopt them. And as Michael and Ivey learned, this form of adoption caters to families that have love in abundance, but not money. By partnering with state agencies, families that offer to care for these needy children are actually provided a stipend to cover costs such as housing, food, and clothing. They are even provided with free health insurance.

The more Michael and Ivey researched the foster system, the more they felt it might work for them. "We felt like we had no more excuses," Michael says. "One thing led to another and my wife and I ended up applying to be foster parents."

After a rigorous, months-long certification process, the Ketterers became licensed foster parents. As a part of the process, Michael and Ivey had to fill out forms that listed the age ranges, genders, and numbers of children they were prepared to care for. Foster-care placements often arise from emergency situations in which multiple children are removed from a dangerous living environment. Potential new caretakers such as the Ketterers must decide in advance whether they could welcome these multiple siblings or take only a single child.

Michael and Ivey were not inclined toward multiples at the time. They were new to foster care, and they feared that taking more than one at a time would overwhelm the family. But their daughter, Sophia, wasn't inclined to agree.

"When we told her we were going to do foster care, she became convinced that she was getting her three little brothers now," Michael says. "I told her that there were little girls who needed families too. We also told Sophia we were only going to take one at a time, but she never seemed to really believe us.

Then the very first call we received from the agency was for three young boys."

All three had been found in a methamphetamine lab hidden in the woods. They had spent their entire lives neglected and had severe behavioral and developmental issues. The many other families the agency had contacted were not able to care for them because of these issues. So although the situation was outside the original parameters the Ketterers had set, the agency decided to call them anyway.

"My daughter had been having these multiple dreams for years about three little boys," Michael says. "When our very first call matched those dreams, we couldn't say no. It would have felt like a complete sin to reject what God so obviously put in our path."

It was for these boys and his other children that Michael decided to enter *America's Got Talent*. Music had always been a part of his life, and stardom had tempted him when he was young. But he had since learned to seek a different reward.

"There was something in me that wanted to be famous," he remembers. "I wanted to become a Christian rock star. Early on I got a call from a record label that wanted to sign me. But then I had this wild dream. I was in heaven, and this person came out of the gates and said, 'Michael, we're so glad you're finally here. We play your music every day.' I realized then that I didn't need a record label to be famous where it matters most."

The Bible frequently declares God's heart for the orphan and the needy. "Treat everyone with justice," God says in one such passage. "Show mercy and tender concern to one another. Do not take advantage of widows. Do not mistreat children whose fathers have died. Do not be mean to outsiders or poor people."[3]

Elsewhere it says,

> The LORD watches over the foreigner
> and sustains the fatherless and the widow.[4]

Verses like these made Michael think that fame in heaven would be based on helping the needy rather than on being a rock star and selling records. He decided to care for what God cares for, to seek the kind of life that would make music in heaven. Having decided they'd rather have fame in heaven than on earth, Michael and his wife chose to foster and then adopt those three boys.

"God knew that there was a season when I would be forty years old, and I would step on the stage and not only sing the song, but I would tell this story. It's been a wild journey. We still go to therapy with my kids every week. We are still in the trenches with each of them. But it's so beautiful because I have seen these boys come into my family and transform in front of my eyes. They went from being orphans to being my sons, my boys. They became Ketterers."

The three boys Michael and Ivey welcomed into their home brought with them serious challenges to their life and family. "We couldn't leave our house for a good six months," Michael says. "They couldn't be trusted out in public. They didn't have running water where they lived before, so we had to teach them how to use the bathroom. We had to teach them to sit at a table and eat dinner. We had to teach them not to cuss us out every time they got angry. We had to teach them so many things. Our life was turned upside down."

With counseling, help from others, and a lot of patience, Michael and Ivey worked through those early troubles. And soon the opportunity came to adopt the boys.

Nearly half the children who enter foster care eventually reunite with their families, but a significant percentage—25 percent in 2018—find a new forever home with an adoptive family.[5]

"The social worker took me and my wife to McDonald's one day," he says. "We sat down at this little table when the boys' mother walked in. She had sunglasses on, and bruises were visible around her neck."

"Would you be willing to adopt my boys?" she asked. "I believe you can give them a better life than I could."

Despite the dire circumstances in which they grew up, the boys were loved. Their mother couldn't properly express that love or give them the care and upbringing they needed. But in this moment, she loved her boys enough to give them up to a better home.

"Yes, absolutely," Michael said to the mother. "We will take these boys."

Their family of three became a family of six by a single declaration from the court.

While caring for their family, Michael also worked as a pediatric nurse. He remembers in particular caring for a seventeen-year-old patient who came in with cerebral palsy.

"If you would ask," he remembers saying to God while caring for this patient, "I would care for a kid with disabilities like this."

That's when Michael got another call from the foster agency.

"We have this little boy," the social worker said. "You are the only qualified nurse in our foster-care system right now. He has cerebral palsy."

Because this child was at risk of being institutionalized and spending his life without the care and love of a family, Michael knew this child's situation called for serious consideration. He suspected God was testing him on his promise.

"I want to bring you this little boy," he felt God say to him. "Rodrigo will preach my good news."

Rodrigo had been born healthy and normal, but when he was just one year old, a caregiver had thrown him into a wall and fractured his skull. The extreme neurological damage had resulted in cerebral palsy.

Doctors listed for the Ketterers all the things Rodrigo would never be able to do. He would never eat without a feeding tube, see, walk, or have a normal relationship. The list of physical and mental limitations seemed endless. Michael and Ivey grappled both with these realities and with God's promise that he would share his good news through Rodrigo.

In the end the Ketterers decided to trust God and agreed to take on Rodrigo. As Ivey focused her attention on their other four children, Michael spent the next several months running Rodrigo to a stream of appointments, therapies, and checkups.

"If we had really known all that would be involved with caring for him, we probably would have said no," he says, looking back. "I remember being at this place of emptiness. I was so tired. I broke down thinking about the commitment we had signed up for. But if we had said no, we would have missed out on so much."

Rodrigo found the love and the specialized care he so badly needed with the Ketterers. As is typical with foster children, a series of court appointments kept Rodrigo and his foster parents connected with the various lawyers and social workers associated with his case. During one such court appointment, Rodrigo brought the entire room to tears.

"This is not the same Rodrigo that we saw," the judge declared. As he came in, Rodrigo had lifted his eyes and verbally greeted the judge. He demonstrated not only speech but sight as well, and he had never been expected to be able to do either. The judge, the lawyers, even the court reporter in the room were weeping.

"Look what you've done," the judge continued. "Look what you did for this little boy."

"I can't take all the credit," Ivey responded. "This little boy was healed by God."

"Praise God," the court reporter said, standing to her feet. "Thank you, Jesus."

This life is full of brokenness and pain, but the good news of Jesus is that he has promised to wipe every tear away and heal every form of brokenness. Even the power of death will ultimately be crushed by the work of Jesus. This is the message of hope that Jesus came to share—the very same message that the courtroom caught a glimpse of in Rodrigo. Jesus has already begun the ultimate healing.

"Every time I tell Roddy's story," Michael says, "his story tells of the good news of Jesus."

Rodrigo, too, eventually became an official member of the Ketterer family.

Then came their sixth child, Sean, who was found homeless on the streets. "He has brought us so much laughter, joy, and fun," Michael says.

"I had this dream of Sean—this little boy," Ivey says. "I thought we were done adopting more. But I told Michael that I think we have one more child coming."

Sure enough God brought them one more gift—their "cherry on top" as they refer to him.

Michael likes to say that the butterfly tells the story of adoption. "When a child comes into the cocoon of love, that safety of family, they are transformed. A metamorphosis takes place."

Michael has lived on both sides of this metamorphosis. As a foster father, he knows what love can do in a child, but he has also struggled with feeling fatherless himself.

"My dad left when I was fourteen years old," he says. "He wasn't completely absent, but he had a lot he was working through. We got put on the back burner."

Perspective and understanding are qualities that come later. When a father leaves, a child only sees his hero drift away. And when that happened to Michael, he was confused and angry. He longed for a father to show him the way. But his father just wasn't there for him.

"I had to look at other people, coaches and teachers, to glean what it means to be a man," he says. "My own father-in-law was an important example for me. But going through that has given me understanding for what my own boys are going through in this moment. They are searching too."

Having to glean the deep truths of life through all these other people made Michael's life feel a little like a journey without a map or compass. But looking back through the years, Michael has seen his heavenly Father guiding his steps.

"It seems ethereal to say that God is our Father," he admits. "But he impacts our lives through his children. He sent me all those people—coaches, pastors, and my father-in-law. When we have had times where Ivey and I worried where money would come from, God has always come through. He will move mountains for you. There was a time when I lost my job and he sent a couple to pay our rent until I could catch up. He has poured out his resources into our life."

Through all the ups and downs of parenting a large family, especially one with so many special needs, Michael and Ivey have learned that God comes through for his children—and not just financially.

"When our heavenly Father looks at us, he doesn't see shame," Michael says. That's something he has come to appreciate in his own parenting, as he has tried to help unwind all the shame and rejection his children carried with them into the family. Even when children become aware of their own behavior issues, they often lack the strength or ability to control themselves. Much patience and care must be poured into them before improvement is seen.

Michael believes that God does that for us too. "Even when we are making really stupid mistakes," he says, "God is not angry with us. His anger is at the darkness that caused the problems. His anger is not at us."

With his unique perspective on patience in the midst of trying parental situations, Michael sheds light on the Father of us all. God sees great things ahead for all his children, even when we are blinded by our circumstances. Patience is his response, and grace is his instinct. He pours out favor when we feel rejected and love when we fear wrath. God is a Father to the fatherless, the lonely, and the cast away.

Michael's stunning audition on *America's Got Talent* won him an immediate pass into the quarterfinals when the panel's toughest judge, Simon Cowell, slammed down the golden buzzer. He was able to introduce his family—and his story—to the world that very night. He continued on in season thirteen of the show, winning praise from judges and fans alike and ending up with a fifth-place finish. As a member of a worship collective called Influence Music, Michael Ketterer witnessed the group's debut album, *Touching Heaven*, reach number 1 on iTunes Christian chart and number 1 on Billboard's Christian Album Sales chart.

In many ways, Jessica Long embodies the dream of every adoptive family. She came to Steve and Beth Long by way of Siberia and is now one of the most decorated female Paralympic athletes alive. But her success in swimming hid her inner struggle to feel whole.

Chapter 10

Whole

feat of gold

JESSICA LONG, PARALYMPIC SWIMMER

Part fish, part human, and all heart, Jessica Long has more Paralympic medals than all but a handful of female athletes ever to grace planet Earth. With twenty-three medals to her name, including thirteen gold, six silver, and four bronze, Jessica is just five short of Olympic legend (and fellow Baltimorean) Michael Phelps. She is a favorite to win in multiple events whenever the next Paralympics take place. (Originally scheduled for the summer of 2020, the Paralympics, along with other worldwide sporting events, are paused indefinitely due to the coronavirus pandemic.) She has high hopes of passing even Phelps's medal count.

Jessica's fierce determination has won her the kind of accolades few ever thought possible. Born with a congenital condition that required the amputation of the lower portion of both her legs, she didn't grow up feeling like she would inspire people. Instead, she grew up angry that she wasn't whole.

"That's the first emotion that comes to mind," Jessica says, thinking of her childhood. "I was always angry with everything that I did. It was a comfortable emotion for me. I didn't even know how to explain why I was angry."

The story of Jessica's early life suggests some reasons why Jessica felt the way she did. Born Tatiana Olegovna Kirillova in Irkutsk, Russia, she was given up for adoption by a teenage mother who feared she would not be able to care for a daughter with special needs. Tatiana then spent the next thirteen months in a Siberian orphanage before being adopted by her American family.

"I'm still amazed when my mom tells me the story of how my dad came to get me," Jessica says. Steve and Beth Long had two children of their own but wished for more. After failing to conceive for nearly a decade, they decided to adopt. They learned about Tatiana in a meeting at their church and knew she belonged in their family. So Steve flew more than seven thousand miles to an obscure corner of Russia. There he met his new daughter and named her Jessica Tatiana Long.

The orphanage told the Longs that Jessica had leg deformities, but it wasn't until after her adoption that a visit to a specialist put a name to her condition. Fibular hemimelia has few treatment options. In less severe cases, special shoes or shoe inserts can correct the discrepancies in leg length that result from missing a portion of the fibula bone. But Jessica lacked nearly all the bones in her lower legs and would never be able to walk without prosthetics.

"They decided to amputate six months after I was adopted,"

she explains. "That way I could be fit into prosthetic legs and learn to walk just like everyone else."

The Long family raised Jessica in their hometown of Baltimore along with Josh, whom they also adopted from Russia. Despite their fertility problems, Steve and Beth went on to have two more children.

It was a happy, loving household. "I didn't feel adopted," Jessica remembers. She pins the source of her anger on another cause. "I was angry that I didn't have legs. I thought maybe that's why my birth mom didn't want me—because I didn't look like a normal person."

Jessica grew up bothered by the inconvenience her body caused those around her. Streams of doctor appointments, piles of extra equipment, and ongoing surgeries made her feel like a burden.

"Every time I grew, I would need to get another surgery," she recalls. Like all prosthetic limbs, having an exact fit is essential to full functionality. The portion of her legs that remained just below the knee continually grew, pushing her prosthetics out of balance.

"I had to get the bone cut back," she remembers. "It was excruciating. I remember being in pain almost my entire childhood. If I got my left leg done, we would have to go back and get the right leg done. Once that was healed, it was time for the left leg again."

"You're not a burden," her parents often reminded her. "But I always felt that way," she says. "It took a lot out of my family getting all those surgeries. It was really tough."

Struggling to feel like she belonged in quite the same way as her siblings, Jessica convinced herself that she would earn her spot.

"It made me very determined," she says. "I think that's why I fell in love with sports. It came naturally to me. I was a really determined athlete."

Jessica's determination earned her a spot as the youngest athlete representing the US in the 2004 Athens Paralympic Games. There she won her first three gold medals at the age of twelve.

"Before an event you have to sit down in a room with your competitors," she recalls. "You enter the call room about twenty minutes before your race. It's intense because you're all after the same thing. You all want that gold medal, but only one person gets it."

There, in the call room, officials examine each competitor's equipment and suit. The roar of the crowd wafts in through the door. The smell of chlorine hangs in the air. It's here, in these hidden moments, that the competition really begins.

Each competitor follows her own strategy for edging out a mental advantage. Some throw stares at their competitors. Others jump around. Jessica prefers to sit with headphones on to push back the flood of adrenaline wanting to run free in her veins. A carefully curated song list plays in her ears, each piece chosen to help her focus without raising her heart rate too much. Released too early into the bloodstream, adrenaline can sap an athlete's energy reserves before a race.

Jessica takes in one breath and then another, mastering the thump-thump of her heart. *This is what I've been training for,* she thinks. *I can win this.*

Currently the world record holder for fourteen different swim races, Jessica Long can, indeed, do it. But she came late to the sport. Her first love was gymnastics.

For six years she trained and later competed in gymnastics events, focusing on the high bar. She performed without the aid of her prosthetics. But walking around on her knees for extended periods of time carries with it the risk of nerve damage, so eventually her parents gave her an ultimatum: continue gymnastics with prosthetics or quit. "I didn't want to wear my legs," she says, "so gymnastics was out of the picture."

She sought another outlet in swimming. Having learned to swim in her grandparents' backyard pool, she loved the freedom of the water.

"I didn't have to wear those heavy prosthetic legs," she says. "When I jumped into the pool, it felt like home to me."

She quickly joined the local swim team at the age of ten. Even without her legs, she outswam able-bodied competitors.

"One day we were at a local swim meet, and one of the officials came over," she recalls. "He said that my times were good enough to qualify for the Paralympics. We had no idea what those were."

Frequently confused with the Special Olympics, which only allows intellectually impaired athletes, the Paralympics is an international competition that welcomes athletes with a range of impairments, both physical and intellectual. Athletes first must prove eligibility in one of ten impairment categories. From there they are classified based on the degree of impairment as it relates to a particular sporting event. Athletes with similar activity limitations compete together to ensure an even playing field.

The Paralympics also differs from the Special Olympics in the way athletes gain entrance to the event. Rather than the random lottery used for the Special Olympics, Paralympics require athletes to qualify in the same way that elite athletes do in the Olympics. They must compete in specific sanctioned events and meet standards of performance to earn a spot on their country's team. There are no participation medals. Only one goes away with the gold.

Jessica was surprised to learn she might compete at such a high level, but she welcomed the chance to prove herself. Proving herself had been a driving force her whole life.

"I remember when my little sister Hannah was born," she says. "I was only four years old, and I was so jealous that she had legs. I couldn't understand what I had done wrong. That was the theme of my life—just being angry, feeling unworthy or like I had done something wrong. I always felt like I hadn't done enough, that I needed to do more."

Jessica's parents took her to church throughout her growing-up years. There she heard of a God who was supposed to love her and had a wonderful plan for her life. But if this plan involved her not having legs, she didn't want anything to do with it.

"God chose us . . . before the world was created," she frequently heard. "He decided long ago to adopt us . . . as his children with all the rights children have."[1]

But for Jessica, adoption was proof of things not going to

plan. If she'd had legs, her mother would not have left her in an orphanage. The fact that she'd needed adopting in the first place only proved that God's plan was not for her.

"Adoption didn't feel like a great thing," she says. "I loved my parents, but I also felt abandoned. So I had a hard time understanding this idea that God wanted to adopt me. I was angry at God, angry for these surgeries, and always in so much pain. When I found swimming, that is where I threw in my frustration and my anger."

Jessica's whole family traveled with her to Greece to watch her compete in her first Paralympic event at age twelve. In her very first event, she became the youngest Paralympian to ever win gold.

"Going into it, I thought this was where I would reach the top and be completely loved, be completely enough," she says. "There was no second, third, or fourth place for me. I always needed to be number one in everything that I did."

But even winning international gold wasn't enough to banish Jessica's sense of not measuring up. "I had a lot of insecurities about being adopted. People would stare at me and my legs. On top of it all, I was born on leap day. So even the calendar skipped over my actual birthday, February 29. I would look at the calendar and think, *Even my birth mom's not thinking about me because the calendar jumped past my birthday.*"

Jessica's determination in sports translated to hardness elsewhere. Masking her feelings of insufficiency, anger permeated her relationships with everyone. She felt broken and weak but displayed nothing but strength and perfection on the outside.

She racked up more medals, signed sponsorships with the likes of Nike, and had her story featured in *Sports Illustrated*. By all other measures she was winning at life. But the more she depended on swimming to define her self-worth, the more alone and isolated she felt.

"I felt unstoppable," she says of the time. "I was more in control of my life than ever. I was on the top of the world in my sport. But I just felt broken, sad, and confused."

Her relationship with God continued to suffer. She blamed him for her legs, for her lost family, and for the twenty-five surgeries she'd endured throughout her childhood. God was supposed to have a wonderful plan for everyone, but none of this seemed wonderful to Jessica.

The more she strove to steer her own ship back to port, the more out to sea she felt. She looked for solace in swimming. She thought that maybe if she won enough, earned enough, or achieved enough, she would find belonging. But all her gold medals added up to a poor substitute for the sense of belonging she needed. Anger dug an ever-deepening hole in her heart.

"Most people thought that I was a Christian," she says. "I went to church on Sundays. I put on a sweet face for everyone else. But at home I was a monster to everyone. I thought I had to earn everyone's love. I thought I had to earn God's love. But that just made me mad. I didn't want anything to do with God."

Jessica always thought that control and achievement was the route to love. She felt if she could master her sport, win that gold, and control all the variables, she could somehow achieve that sense of belonging she craved. But by the time she competed in the 2012 London Games, she learned she couldn't control any of the things that mattered.

"It was about six months before the Games that I talked with a Russian reporter about the idea of finding my birth mom," she says. "I didn't even share that with my family because I thought they would be upset. I still felt like I had to earn their love. But then, while competing at the London Games, I learned that my birth family had been found in Russia."

When Jessica heard that her parents had been found, she had to confront the anger she felt toward them.

"I didn't want to deal with it," she says. "I didn't understand why my birth mom was coming into my life. I didn't even know if I wanted this. I was upset with her and wasn't ready to forgive her for putting me up for adoption. Her coming into my life was not what I had planned. It changed everything.

"I'd overcome twenty-five surgeries, walking in prosthetics, hours and hours of practice and elite training. I had done everything on my own. In a sense I felt on top of the world. And yet there was so much I couldn't control—including my anger, my happiness, or even when my mother came back into my life."

A decision confronted Jessica at this point. She had held on to control of her life for so long. Her iron determination had forced out win after win in swimming. But it had done nothing for her relationships. No matter what she won in the pool, it didn't change how she felt on the inside or whether others loved her. She realized she could never earn her way into her birth family, her adoptive family, or even God's family. She simply couldn't control these things.

"I had always thought I could do anything, but now I realized that I couldn't do it alone anymore. I needed to give up control."

About that time, Jessica went to a Friday night Bible study with a friend. Someone asked, "Does anyone want to accept Christ into your heart?"

She had heard these words countless times before, but this evening she finally understood. You don't earn your way into God's family; you accept his invitation.

"I had been holding on to everything so tightly," she remembers. "Now, hearing that invitation, something just seemed to let loose in me. I stood up, and for the first time in my entire life I felt enough. I can't really explain it. It was this amazing feeling of knowing that angels were rejoicing that I was actually a part of God's family. I had never felt fulfillment like that from winning gold medals and sponsorships. It was all just fleeting. It wasn't happiness. It wasn't joy. Not like this."

Within a year of learning that her Russian family had been found, Jessica was approached by NBC about flying to Russia to meet them. Jessica, her sister Hannah, and a film crew traveled to see the places where she had spent her first year of life. She struggled with waves of emotions, still learning to allow feelings other than strength and confidence show on her face.

"I had communicated with my birth family on Facebook, and I'd seen pictures at this point, but I didn't know what to expect when I actually met them. No matter how much you prepare, you can't prepare for what it's like to meet your birth family."

By now she knew the outlines of the story. Natalia and Oleg, only seventeen and eighteen at the time, had been unwed, poor, and without the support of family when they discovered the severe birth defects of their baby. Their small Siberian village had no support systems for such circumstances, and the medical professionals there insisted they would not be able to give her the care she needed.[2] So they had reluctantly given her up to an orphanage eighteen hours away by train. Giving up their firstborn child had been traumatic, but they'd still ended up marrying and building a family together. They had three other children, including Dasha, who was also disabled and who was cared for at home.

"I had dreamed of my birth family my entire life, since I was a little girl," Jessica recalls. "Now I was about to meet them. But once we got to Russia, I doubted myself. What if my birth family didn't want to see me?"

They began the trip with a visit to her orphanage. The woman who had handed her to her father so many years before still worked there. She proudly showed the pool they had at the orphanage and talked about how much she and everyone else at the orphanage admired all that Jessica had achieved.

"We went outside to do an interview for the cameras, and I just started to cry. It was one of the first times I truly believed just how loved I was by my parents in Baltimore. They had come all the way over here to find me."

Following the orphanage visit, they took an eighteen-hour overnight train to Irkutsk, where she would finally meet her birth family. People stood on their roofs to catch a glimpse of the camera crew and the girl who had finally returned. Jessica gripped her sister's hand as she walked toward a little blue house. As she turned toward the door, her parents came out with tears coursing down their cheeks.

"My daughter! My daughter!" Natalia said between sobs of joy. Both she and Oleg wept for joy, hugging and kissing their long-lost child. They moved inside, where Jessica met her two sisters and her brother. Her mother shared how she had never forgiven herself for giving Jessica up.

"It was in that moment that I realized that God had forgiven me my whole life," Jessica says. "If he had done that for me, then I could forgive my mother too. I wasn't angry with her. I could see that what she did was brave, hoping for a better life for me."

As Jessica looks back through the story of her life now, she can finally see the plan that God had all along. She didn't lose a family; she gained a new one.

"I'm so proud of my name," she says. "I'm Jessica to my family in Baltimore. And I'm Tatiana to my family in Russia. Altogether I am Jessica Tatiana Long."

But Jessica has also found a home in the family of God. Entrance wasn't gained by winning gold, behaving in church, or racking up enough good deeds. God chose her before the foundation of the world. He chose her because he loves her.

"He's there all the time," she says. "When I'm struggling and when I'm having good days, he still loves me. For so many years I swam with so much anger and hurt. But now I'm not angry. I swim because I love the sport."

Jesus once told a story describing the family of God.[3] It began with a son who left home and took with him much of his father's riches. He wasted it all on wild living and parties, until finally the money ran out. The son had squandered everything. He became destitute, struggling to find food enough to eat. He even lent himself out to work at a nearby pig farm, where he stole meals out of the pig slop.

In that low moment, the son thought back to the father he had left. He didn't think he could return home, not as a son anyway. But as he reflected on his situation, he realized that his father's servants were at least well fed. If he could not return home as a son, perhaps he could return as a servant.

He traveled back home, convinced his father could never want him as a son. He didn't deserve that. He had let his father down. But then his father spotted the shamefaced young man walking back home. Filled with joy, the father ran, threw his arms around him, and said, "My son."

God is this type of Father. He has a plan for your life, just as the father in Jesus' story had plans for his son. But when the son abandoned his father's plans and squandered everything, the father never ceased to love him. He still considered him his son.

If you are still trying to earn your way into God's arms, consider the story of Jessica and consider the story Jesus told. No matter how hard you try, you won't earn your way into God's affections. You can't—because he already loves you and has already invited you to join. He loved you long before you were born. He has loved you in the midst of every mistake, error, and sin. He has loved you, does love you, and will love you.

You just have to accept it.

in search of
Friendship

God speaks through people.

Through the ages, they have been his favorite medium. Rarely does he pop out of heaven and descend with lightning and a booming voicing saying, "Here I am. It's God." Instead, he speaks through the quiet voices of his followers. He has spoken through exiled shepherds and wandering nomads. It was human song makers and poets who recorded so many of his promises from old. God chose widows, farmers, fishermen, and tax collectors as his agents in the Bible. Even when the Son of God came to earth, he first dressed himself in human flesh and became one of us.

It's among these weak vessels that he sifts for the faithful. He isn't looking for those who are merely cowed into believing or chased into his arms by fear. He seeks those earnest enough to hear his whispers over the din of earthly distractions.

But who God chooses to speak through is not always who the world would choose. In fact, he warns us many times in the Bible that he does not judge people like we do. He is not impressed with beauty, strength, or the number of Instagram followers. He does not care about money or prestige.

God judges the heart. He looks for humility, kindness, faith, and a willingness to serve. It's through people with these quiet inner strengths that God makes the most noise. It's through their lips that his voice is most often heard. Then, as now, he chooses the simple to confound the wise and the weak to humble the strong. Today, as much as in any other age, God speaks through the unexpected.

He speaks through strangers, associates, and friends if you have ears to hear him. In the pages to come, you'll find the stories of some of those humble messengers and the people whose lives they touched. Through them maybe you'll hear him calling out to you too.

Chapter 11

Reborn

a prince with no father

REMI ADELEKE, ACTOR

Born a privileged African prince but raised poor on the streets of the Bronx, Remi Adeleke spent much of his life trying to fill the void left by the death of his father. Decades later, he would realize the many people his Father in heaven had sent to guide his path to a new kind of life.

Remi is the son of Chief Adebayo Adeleke of the Yoruba tribe in southwest Nigeria. This powerful tribe has been the dominant cultural and political force in the region for more than a thousand years. Numbering nearly forty million people today, the Yoruba tribe is a composite of multiple smaller ethnic groups, each with its own ancestral lands, traditions, and set of rulers.

The chiefs of the Yoruba tribe—the Oba, as they are known locally—lost their political power with the coming of colonial and, more recently, democratic institutions. But their status as cultural icons and as people of influence lingers into modernity. Remi's father, known simply as Chief by many, took his role as a cultural leader for his people seriously.

"My first priority is to my country," Chief would often say to those who questioned his grand ideas for the future of his people. "I cannot abandon Nigeria, even in the smallest way."

Possessing a sharp mind, a bold vision for the future, and a passionate love for his nation—as well as professional training as an engineer and architect—Chief built a sprawling business empire. He hoped to modernize and showcase to the world the beauty and genius of his people. His incredible wealth led also to an ever-growing sphere of influence, landing him a seat on the boards of the prestigious World Teleport Association in London and the New York World Trade Center.

But overshadowing the noble ideals and endeavors of men like Chief Adebayo Adeleke was a notoriously corrupt government. Chief leveraged his fortunes and life ambitions into a massive real-estate project—actually a manmade island just offshore in Lagos—now known as Banana Island. But he lost everything when the Nigerian government seized the land, and he passed away shortly afterward. Bitten by a rabid dog in Lagos, he died from a combination of the rabies itself and an adverse reaction to the medication prescribed to treat it.

Remi, his older brother, Bayo, and their American mother, Pauline, were staying in New York at the time. Pauline flew to Nigeria for the funeral, where she was informed of the complete loss of the family fortune by John, Remi's half brother.

"He poured every dime he had into the project," John told her. "*All* of his finances. There's nothing left."

Transformed overnight from a rich prince of the mighty Yoruba tribe to the impoverished five-year-old son of a newly single mother, Remi would grow up in a world very different from his father's. "I can't tell you much about the land of my birth," he says. "But I can tell you all about the Bronx. I love the Bronx, both the good and the bad."

Remi grew up in the very neighborhood that birthed the modern hip-hop movement, just about the time when hip-hop was springing into the national consciousness. The newly burgeoning genre of music had roots in the block parties popular among African Americans in the Bronx during the 1960s and 1970s. DJs at these parties would string together popular songs using percussive interludes combined with their own rhythmic lyrics. These interludes extended to become their own wildly popular musical genre. By the time of Remi's youth, hip-hop pounded from every stereo on his block.

"It was in the streets, blasting from the houses," Remi recalls. "Gangsta rap got huge, and it really caught on with me."

Much of early hip-hop had focused on themes of social, political, and economic justice and the struggles of African American people. But a subgenre, popularly known as gangsta (gangster) rap, idealized the darker undercurrents of society, including violence, promiscuity, drugs, and materialism. And something in that music called to the young Remi. It was art he could relate to.

Throughout his childhood, Remi's mother had worked to

instill in him an appreciation for the arts in general and especially the work of African and African American artists. The family made frequent visits to the museums of New York, including the Schomburg Center for Research in Black Culture, the Studio Museum in Harlem, and the Lehman College Art Gallery. His mother had also introduced them to theater and film, and their many trips between Broadway and the Bronx not only gave Remi a love for plays and movies but would later whet his appetite for acting.

Remi appreciated the arts his mom exposed him to, including the museum visits. "They gave me depth," he remembers, "showed me the immense creativity of Black people, and kept me connected to my African heritage. But they didn't give me the hope that I found in hip-hop." The art he found booming in the streets seemed to offer what his heart longed for.

A father.

"Though I wasn't aware of it at the time," Remi reflects, "the night when I first grieved over my father had been the first step of a journey to find the treatment for my wounds and fill my paternal void. That's what led me to the art of hip-hop."

"In my mind, the artists I listened to had come from where I came from," he says. "They had single moms, grew up in the inner city. I felt like I could relate to them. I wanted to dress like them, walk like them, talk like them, think like them. I wanted to gain the same level of attention from women as they did. They became my fathers. While some dads use a ball to play catch with their sons, I used rhymes and beats to play catch with the 'dad' I found in hip-hop. I fell in love with him. I fell in love with his display, his confidence, his allure, his portrayal of rags to riches, and his conspicuous representatives, the rappers. I wanted to follow in his footsteps."

Remi never actually aspired to be a hip-hop artist himself. But as he grew, his goals gradually crystallized in the image of his heroes: money, then power, then respect.

The trouble was, he didn't have any money.

"I was desperate to get the things my mom couldn't afford to get me," Remi admits. "Theft would define the beginnings of my hustle."

He started out small, stealing money first from his mother, then from local bodegas. He even stole his mother's engagement ring, which had been given to her by his dead father.

"I was always able to figure out creative ways to steal," Remi says. "By the time I was nineteen, I had money, cars, women. I'm a thug. I'm a gangsta. I'm a player. You can't tell me nothing. I got all the money. My dress was just like those I saw in the music videos. My hat was on backward. My jeans were sagging. My attitude was just cocky and arrogant. I was trying to live up to the standard of these rappers, these gangsters, these hustlers. I was totally out of control."

Stealing led to dealing. He joined a couple of friends selling drugs upstate. But that venture failed to give him the kind of life he wanted. "I had big dreams of launching a record company," Remi says. "But that dream would require a lot more money than I was bringing in." So he took a job at a cell-phone company and developed a hustle that promised to bring him the income he wanted.

The new job tasked him with selling cell phones by cold-calling potential clients. But a coworker quickly showed Remi how to game the system by using stolen identities to open new lines of credit. For each stolen identity, he could register three new phones, earning a commission on the sale and then selling the new phones on the streets.

"In the first week I rang up $4,000 in illegal sales, plus the commissions on them," Remi says. "I had never seen that much money in my life."

He found a particularly lucrative niche with drug dealers, who required the kind of anonymity his hustle specialized in. One such illicit client, Devan, eventually asked him for twenty or twenty-five phones per week.

Remi hesitated at that point. "I had been trying to limit my weekly total, just to be safe," he says. "Selling this many to a single person would change the plan." But the promise of such a huge influx of weekly cash proved too tempting to reject.

The process for each cell phone was the same. It would be registered to a line of credit associated with a stolen identity. But with the account holder completely unaware of the transaction, no payment would ever be made. A collection process would then unfold, and after three months the cell phone's service would be shut off for lack of payment. Then Remi's customers would come back for another phone.

The process worked great.

Until it didn't.

One day Remi opened the door of his mother's apartment to a particularly angry—and likely armed—Devan. The cell phones

Remi had sold him just two weeks before had already shut off, and he wanted his money back.

"This was a huge problem," Remi admits. "Having the phones shut off after weeks instead of months meant that someone at my company might have caught on to my hustle. And if that was the case, I was looking at time in federal prison."

"I'm going to give you one week," Devan said. "If you don't have my money by next week, things are not going to go well for you."

Devan didn't need to spell it out. Remi understood that the gun likely hidden beneath Devan's coat wouldn't stay out of sight the next time he visited.

"I was confronted with a huge wake-up call," Remi says. "What made the situation even worse was the fact that he had threatened me at my mom's house, a few feet from where she was sleeping."

Remi spent the next twenty-four hours scrounging up the cash to repay Devan. And even as he handed over the money, he knew his cell-phone hustle was over. Someone would soon be after him—if not Devan, it would be the feds. So he got out of the cell-phone business before it was too late.

Where has my life gone to? he found himself thinking. But then he remembered something his mother had told him whenever she caught wind of his antics.

"You need to remember who you are," she'd said. "This is not you. You're a prince, a part of the Yoruba tribe. You're not a thief. You need to live up to your tribe and to your name."

Adeleke.

To most who heard it in the Bronx, the name sounded African but otherwise ordinary. But Nigerians knew the extraordinary power that lay in those syllables. *Ade* means "crown," and *leke* means "above." Together they announce that "the king triumphed."

"In English and American culture, we refer to royalty as king and queen," Remi explains. "African culture is different. Royalty is referred to as chief or is designated by the last name. My grandfather was a chief of the Yoruba tribe and started the Adeleke name. Because my grandfather was a chief and my dad was the firstborn son, also a chief, the royal blood runs down to me, my brothers and sisters, and my sons."

Remembering his mother's words and his name called Remi to a different and higher way of living. But he still didn't know where to turn next.

Then one day, while lying in bed, he heard a voice saying, "Join the military."

He sat up.

He saw no one. The voice sounded far away and dreamlike, but it rang clear to his soul, even as the objections rose in his mind.

"For me to join the military was like joining the enemy," he explains. "I associated anybody in a uniform with the police. And I hated cops."

Remi's attitude toward people in uniform was understandable, especially in 1990s New York. These were the years when the infamous stop-and-frisk policies gained widespread use. These policies gave police authority to temporarily detain, question, and search any citizen they suspected of illegal activity—including those they simply encountered on the streets. And in practice, unfortunately, the burden of these policies fell disproportionately on people of color.

Of the 125,000 pedestrian stops recorded from January 1998 through March 1999, 51 percent were Black and 33 percent were Hispanic—populations that represented only 26 percent and 24 percent of the city's population respectively. Minority people were up to 2.5 times as likely to be stopped than White people— this despite the fact that minorities actually had a lower arrest rate than White people in these encounters,[1] meaning when they were stopped, they were less likely to have actually done anything illegal.

Not surprisingly, the frequent stops of mostly minority people eroded the community trust so necessary in effective police work. This mistrust was magnified further by incidents like the 1997 beating and sodomizing of Abner Louima by a group of police officers in Brooklyn and the 1998 killing of Amadou Diallo, whom police officers shot nineteen times after mistaking his wallet for a gun.

Such incidents led many minority New Yorkers like Remi to distrust and even hate the police. And Remi's misgivings had taken on a more personal meaning when he was arrested for refusing to leave a McDonald's after he had purchased a meal. "I had always assumed that I would one day end up in a jail cell," Remi admits. "But it was quite humorous, considering all the bad I did, that the police arrested me for a Big Mac, French fries, and a Sprite."

But as Remi now sat in his bed thinking through all his objections, he realized he still needed to pay attention to the voice he had heard. "I did not want to join the military, but this voice guided me," he says. "I left the house. I walked into the recruiter's office, and within a week I was in navy boot camp. It happened that fast."

Why the navy? Ironically, it was Remi's love for movies that nudged him in that direction. His favorites films as a teen had been director Michael Bay's action thrillers. Now he found more specific inspiration in a Michael Bay movie called *The Rock*, which featured a team of Navy SEALs who fight and sneak their way into the prison at Alcatraz to rescue a group of hostages and defuse some missiles. (Remi would later discover that several of the actors in *The Rock* were actual Navy SEALs.)

Watching *The Rock*, Remi found himself relating to someone in uniform for the first time. He thought of those men as he walked into the recruiter's office to join the navy—only to discover that joining wouldn't be easy.

"I had a record," Remi explains. "The decisions in my past disqualified me for where I wanted to go in the future. But Tiana Reyes, the navy recruiter I met that day, advocated for me. She played a pivotal role in getting me into the navy despite my background."

Although Remi still dreamed of becoming a SEAL, his physical and mental aptitude scores weren't high enough at first to qualify him for SEAL training. It took persistence and hard work for him to earn his way into the SEAL program. Even then, something seemed missing in his life.

"SEAL training is like nothing on this planet," Remi says. "But even though I went to SEAL training and it was a positive influence on my life, that paternal void was still there. I still continued to search."

Then Remi met a woman named Cecilia. "She was like a breath of fresh air," Remi remembers. "It was like the world just completely stopped. When she invited me to church, I knew I'd do whatever I needed to do to get close to her."

The relationship grew deeper. Cecilia waited for him when he went away on deployment and cared for him when he came home injured. But training for an elite military group like the SEALs worked on Remi's ego. Restless and more than a little prideful, he started to question his commitment to Cecilia.

I'm about to be a SEAL, he thought. *Why would I want to be tied down?*

"Cecilia did absolutely nothing to warrant me breaking up with her, and I knew that, but at the time I didn't care. I wanted to be with other women and not do it behind her back. It was all about me, me, me, me, me!"

Remi would later find himself in cold-weather survival training in Alaska. His time in the cold and barren wilderness woke him to how he had treated so many people.

"It was completely silent out there," he recalls. "I began to think about how I had treated my mom and Cecilia and other people I claimed I loved. I still yearned for that paternal presence too. I couldn't really sleep, and then I began to have suicidal thoughts. I was at the lowest point I had ever been in my entire life."

At that point he knew nothing about the Bible beyond the simple fact of Jesus. But with that simple ounce of faith, he cried out: "Help me, Jesus! Help me!"

Remi cried out to God not really knowing what that would mean for his life. He returned from Alaska determined to be a better person but not yet a committed follower of Jesus. He apologized to Cecilia and begged her to take him back. She refused. But what she did agree to would lead him back to Jesus.

"If you won't take me back," Remi said to her, "can you take me to church?"

She did.

"I just humbled myself," Remi remembers. "I submitted my life to Jesus because I knew a change had to take place. I gave my life to the Lord. That was the day I was pulled out of my darkness and into God's light.

"I know that God didn't intend for me to be a thug. I know that God didn't intend for me to be a hustler and a player, to dress the way I dressed and to talk the way I talked. He didn't intend that for me. Now I can honestly say that I'm not just a product of my environment. I'm a product of Jesus Christ."

From that point on, Remi began to surround himself with other believers "who didn't just read the Bible but actually *lived* the Bible." He began to pray as well. "All I wanted to do was be with Jesus and forsake that life that I used to live and live this new life with Jesus. My whole life dramatically changed."

Though Cecilia never took Remi back as a boyfriend, he became determined to be the man he had failed to be before. In Jesus he'd finally found a role model and a father figure who showed him a path to peace, redemption, and purpose. The changes in his heart led to changes in how he served as a SEAL, eventually leading him to be selected as the SEAL of the year in the Naval Special Warfare community.

As Jesus transformed Remi's heart and mind, he also gave him another shot at love. In May 2011, Jessica and Remi met online and had their first date soon afterward.

"This may sound corny, but that night I fell in love with her! Not because of her story per se or because of how she looked, but because we both were able to see past all the outward things of life and see each other's hearts."

Remi soon decided to leave the military and marry Jessica. The plan was for him to stay home with their future children and also develop a speaking career. But once again, he ran into some obstacles.

"I was expecting to have all these opportunities for speaking engagements," Remi says. "But the phones didn't ring. I got really nervous because I had only about six months of savings. I have a wife and she's pregnant with our first son, but we're barely scraping by."

Then he got a call he never could have expected. Michael Bay, the same director whose movie had inspired Remi to become a Navy SEAL, was making a film called *Transformers: The Last Knight*, and he needed a background extra to play the part of a special-forces soldier. The opportunity would later land Remi a principal role in the film. This has led to more opportunities in acting, speaking, and writing—including the publication of his memoir *Transformed: A Navy SEAL's Unlikely*

Journey from the Throne of Africa, to the Streets of the Bronx, to Defying All Odds.

"When you look at my story, going from the Bronx to the military and then to special operations, being a husband and a father, and now having a career in acting, there's only one way to sum it up," Remi says. "It's God. He's been with me throughout my entire life. He's seen the good, the bad, and the ugly, and he has used it all to bring me to where I am today."

"I don't want to force things anymore. I just want to allow God to do whatever it is that he wants to do in my life. If he wants to take me out of this acting career next week, then so be it. If he wants me to get back into the military, so be it. I have learned that God's plan is better than any plan that I could ever have."

The early death of his father left a hole in Remi's life. Who could set a path for Remi to follow? When Remi needed to make a decision, who could he go to for help? When Remi needed someone to have his back or advocate for him, who could step in? And who would remind Remi that he is a prince and not a thief?

It was only in hindsight that Remi saw that God had been the father he'd always needed. It was the voice of his heavenly Father that directed him to the navy when he needed a path. It was his heavenly Father who brought him to just the right recruiter when he needed an advocate. And it is his heavenly Father who the Bible says has "chosen those who are poor in the eyes of the world to be rich in faith and to inherit the kingdom he promised those who love him."[2]

Remi is a prince of Africa and now also a prince of the kingdom of heaven. But it's the latter title that he now orients his life around. It's a title available to all who choose to love and follow God. But like all titles of such nature, it comes with a responsibility.

Have you found hope in Jesus? Have you been given new life or purpose in following him? Have you found love when Jesus came into your life?

Then you, too, are an heir to the throne of the kingdom of God and bound by the responsibility of that title.

"You are the light of the world," Jesus once said to those who represent his kingdom. "Let your light shine before others, that they may see your good deeds and glorify your Father in heaven."[3]

God uses people like you to shine his light into the darkness. Light does not fear the darkness; it overcomes it. Let it shine in your life, and let it shine into the lives of those you encounter.

You never know. The light you share may end up reaching an audience of millions.

That's exactly what happened when Augusta, a housemaid from Brazil, came to work for one of the biggest names in Hollywood.

Chapter 12
Maid

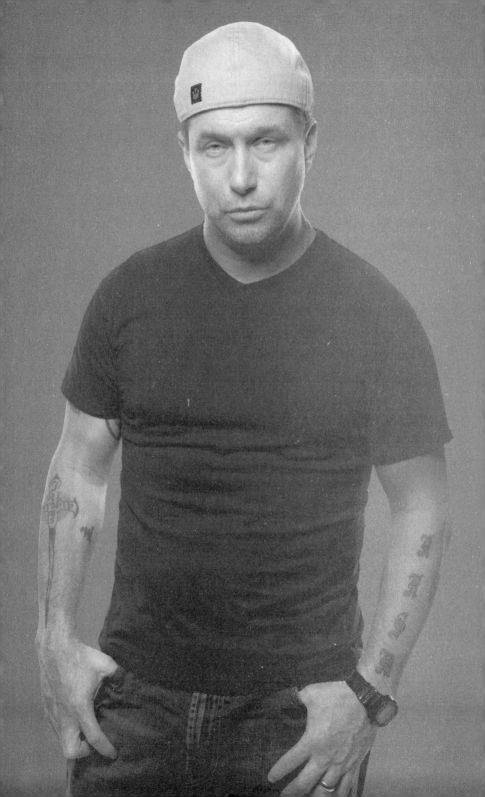

a friend made all the difference

STEPHEN BALDWIN, ACTOR

Have you heard the story of God speaking through a donkey?

It's true.

A few thousand years ago, there was a man named Balaam who would not listen to God.[1]

Balaam was a prophet for hire. For the right price he would grant blessings or bring down curses. And one day, the king of his land sent for him to curse an enemy.

"Do not curse them," God instructed Balaam, to his great surprise.

But Balaam eventually agreed to go with the king's men, and God became angry. He sent a message in the form of a deadly angel with sword in hand who stood in the road to block Balaam's way. But the great prophet never saw the angel. Only the donkey

Balaam was riding succeeded in deciphering the deadly message. When the donkey ran off the path to escape the threatening angel, Balaam beat and cursed him.

"What have I done to you to make you beat me?" the donkey said.

"You have made a fool of me!" Balaam stormed in response, seemingly unsurprised that the donkey was speaking his language. "If only I had a sword in my hand, I would kill you right now."

"Have I been in the habit of disobeying you like this?" the donkey argued.

"No" is all Balaam managed before suddenly he saw what the donkey had seen from the first: an angel of death with sword drawn, hemming them in.

"If the donkey had not turned away," the angel said to Balaam, "I would certainly have killed you."

So often, when God speaks, we fail to see the angels he sends—or, perhaps, the donkeys. We don't see the truth in the advice of a friend, the guidance of a mentor, or, in the case of Stephen Baldwin, the words of a housemaid.

Stephen began his acting career in television, eventually starring in shows like *The Young Riders*. After finding roles in numerous smaller or independent films, he landed his breakthrough movie role in *The Usual Suspects*, which went on to win the Academy Award for Best Original Screenplay. But as his professional life soared, Stephen's personal life fell in the opposite direction.

"Unbeknown to me at the time, my life before Christ was a totally day-in and day-out existence of self-absorbance," Stephen admits. "I just did what you'd normally do when trying to maintain a career in the movie business, the Hollywood treadmill of life. I was very much swept up in that existence."

A prolific actor with scores of big- and small-screen credits to his name stretching through three decades, Stephen became a household name starting in the mid-1990s. But no amount of Hollywood success could win him satisfaction.

"What's weird about the movie business is that it's so obsessive you can't see it when you're in it," he says. "Satisfaction isn't even something you consider. But I began realizing that for me it was not satisfying at all. I was missing the incredible presence that I have now of peace, the understanding that God runs my life and not me."

Stephen had grown up Roman Catholic but had left the faith as soon as he was old enough to make his own decisions. "I found the whole experience rather meaningless," he says. "When I turned thirteen, I walked away from any type of Christian experience."

Once he stopped practicing faith, he quickly dove into drugs and alcohol. By the time of his role in *The Usual Suspects*, Stephen says he had "snorted enough cocaine to throw the entire population of a small South American country into anaphylactic shock."[2]

It wasn't until his wife hired a cleaning woman from Brazil that Stephen heard the voice of God calling him back.

In 1987 Stephen had met Brazilian graphic designer Kennya Deodato. The two married shortly afterward and had two daughters, Alaia and Hailey. To help with the daily housework of raising the young girls, Kennya hired a woman from her hometown of Rio de Janeiro.

But the woman came to their Arizona home with a mission of her own. No matter what chore she took on, she sang. And a common theme repeated through each song, whether she cooked, cleaned, or helped with the baby.

"Have you noticed what she sings about in every song?" Kennya finally complained to Stephen.

"What is it?"

"Jesus," she whispered. It wasn't a word that came easily in that household. They used it in swearing or in anger, sure. But to say the name like it meant something real felt freakish just by association. Religion couldn't have been further from either of their minds. Having a full-blown Christian singer as a housemaid seemed weird beyond all words.

A few days passed as Kennya contemplated what to do with this endless string of Jesus songs.

"I noticed your singing," she finally said to the woman. "And I was curious: Why is every song about Jesus? Maybe there's another tune in your repertoire, so to speak."

Augusta was the woman's name. She stopped what she was doing and burst into a belly-shaking laugh.

"I'm your boss!" Kennya responded with annoyance. "What's so funny?"

Augusta composed herself. "I don't mean to be disrespectful, but I'm laughing because you think the only reason I'm here is to clean your house."

"You're scaring me," Kennya said. "What do you mean?"

"For me to go to America for the first time and work for complete strangers was a very big life decision," Augusta shared. "So I did what I always do whenever I make big decisions in my life. I went to church, spoke with my pastor, and prayed with my friends."

She went on to explain that she had received a prophecy in answer to her prayer. The word *prophecy* sounded as bewildering to Kennya as a six-sided circle. But Augusta insisted she had received her prophetic answer during a prayer meeting at church.

A group had gathered, with each person sharing a prayer request. Augusta was struggling with the decision to move to America, which meant leaving family, friends, and everyone she'd ever known. If it was God's plan for her life, she'd go. She just needed to know what God wanted.

As everyone began praying, a lady came over to Augusta with a prophecy. "I think I've heard from God about your situation," she said.

"Stephen, I need to tell you why Augusta says she has come to our home," Kennya reported later. "She says the real reason she's here is that you and I are going to become born-again Christians."

She paused as they both shared a look of incredulity.

"And at some point after that, we're going to have our own ministry."

Stephen could only stammer in disbelief at the absurdity of the statement.

"Just to hear that idea vocalized at that point in time was utterly ridiculous," Stephen recalls. He had just started his role in *The Young Riders*. The Western television series would eventually lead to his being cast in several career-making films.

"I was literally embarking on one of the biggest breaks in my career," he says. "I was making more money than I could ever imagine. But that really was the beginning of my spiritual journey for me."

Augusta only stayed with the Baldwins a short time. But in the year and a half she worked in their home, she and Kennya became good friends. In time, Kennya began to listen more seriously to the good news of Jesus that Augusta sang about so often. They even began studying the Bible and praying together. When the Baldwins moved back to Stephen's home state of New York, Kennya and Augusta began attending church together.

"Sure enough, it wasn't too long after that that Kennya became an extremely intense committed believer in Jesus Christ," Stephen says.

"Honey, sit down," he remembers Kennya saying to him after one of the church services. "I've accepted Jesus Christ as my Lord and Savior. What I need to do each day, to the best of my ability, is to become the most obedient servant to Jesus that I can. I don't know what you're going to do, but that's what I'm going to do."

The change that followed in Kennya's life astounded Stephen.

My wife's a Jesus freak, he thought to himself at the time. She immediately began a daily regimen of Bible study and prayer. She attended church and began to see new purpose in her life.

"I became curious about the authenticity of her experience," Stephen says. "I saw firsthand that she became tremendously committed to her prayer life and her studying of the Bible. As I was pondering why all this was happening to her, the terrorist attacks of 9/11 happened."

On September 11, 2001, nineteen men associated with the Islamic terrorist group al-Qaeda boarded four separate planes. Once in the air, the men proceeded to hijack the various planes. At 8:45 a.m. they slammed the first of these planes, a Boeing 767 topped off with twenty thousand gallons of jet fuel, into the north tower of the World Trade Center in downtown Manhattan.

Media immediately began reporting that a plane had struck one of New York's tallest skyscrapers. The theories at the time called the incident a "freak attack." Eighteen minutes after the first plane hit, with television studios broadcasting live the images of the flame-engulfed building, a second plane streamed across televisions around the world. United Airlines Flight 175 turned sharply and crashed into the south tower on live television.

An hour later, at 9:45 a.m., terrorists slung another plane into the west side of the Pentagon, headquarters of the US Department of Defense. One hundred people died on impact, in addition to the sixty-four people on the flight.

Passengers and crew aboard the fourth plane caught wind of the earlier attacks. Seeking to halt another disaster, they fought against their hijackers. In the tumult, the plane sped out of control and crashed into a field near Shanksville, Pennsylvania.

In all, 2,996 people perished in the attacks. Causing more deaths than even the attack on Pearl Harbor that launched America into World War II, 9/11 changed the nation—and it also changed Stephen Baldwin.

"I didn't think something like that was possible," Stephen remembers. "It couldn't happen in America, not in New York in 2001."

But it did happen. And Stephen began thinking that the impossible was possible.

When Augusta came into his home singing about Jesus and talking about a prophecy that he and Kennya would become "born-again Christians," it had sounded absurd and impossible. But the world was changing. The absurd was happening. And he saw the impossible happening in the events of the world, but also in his wife.

If what they say about Jesus Christ is true, he thought, *then he could come back tomorrow and then the game's over.*

For the first time in his life he began contemplating the real meaning of life and what might come after it. "I started to seriously pursue who I was," he says, "and what life was about. I wondered what the Christian faith could look like if I really focused on it."

He'd toyed with Christianity as a child. But what he'd experienced then had just been religion and tradition at best. But when he saw the transformation of his wife, his curiosity had risen to the level of opening the Bible and attempting prayer. Now he wondered what would happen if he went all in with God.

"I came to a place of willingness," he says. "I decided to walk this walk of faith in Jesus Christ for myself. I was going to do this thing as obediently as I could according to the Bible. I decided to give it my all. It's been fascinating to see that the message Augusta brought to me and my wife has come true—completely beyond anything I could wildly imagine."

Stephen and Kennya are still surrounded by the type of Hollywood doubters they once were themselves. He is well aware that something strange and supernatural has occurred in him.

"It's available to everybody, but not everybody is willing to be obedient to it," he says. "It's like the story of when Nicodemus came to talk with Jesus."

A leading religious scholar, Nicodemus came to Jesus seeking answers. He had listened to many of Jesus' teachings but struggled to grasp the concepts.[3]

Jesus described what Nicodemus lacked: "You must be born again," he said.

This only confused Nicodemus more. How could an old man like himself go back into his mother and start life all over?

"People give birth to people," Jesus clarified, "but the Spirit gives birth to spirit." He was saying that Nicodemus didn't need another physical birth. He needed a spiritual birth.

"The wind blows where it wants to," Jesus added. "You hear the sound it makes. But you can't tell where it comes from or where it is going. It is the same with everyone who is born with the Spirit."

It's this invisible and incomprehensible presence in his life that Stephen has found so compelling.

"The presence of the Spirit of God inside of me and in my life is something that I have never been able to even remotely experience anywhere else in life—not in Hollywood, not in success, not in anything. Jesus referenced how you don't know where the wind is coming from and you don't know where it's going. That's how faith works with God. If tomorrow God had me pack up the wife and kids, sell the house, and do this or that, and if I knew it was the Holy Spirit communicating to me, then I would absolutely do it."

Stephen's story is not the hit-rock-bottom-and-come-to-Jesus story that others have experienced. While he struggled with drugs and alcohol for many years, he found help in a twelve-step program and became sober many years before finding Jesus. His professional career hadn't fallen apart, forcing him to crawl back to God for help. His marriage hadn't collapsed, leaving him alone and searching. Instead, he was wooed by the promises of true satisfaction in Jesus. As great as his life was, Jesus offered a better one.

"Most people assume that I hit bottom and had nowhere else to turn and that's why I became a Christian," he explains. "But my life was awesome. I just didn't realize it could be better."

"The Spirit of God within me is constantly speaking to me. He allows me, emotionally and psychologically, to not have any fear about life or my existence because it's not mine. It is God's life in me for him to do with what he wants. My walk of faith has become more of a wild ride for me than I ever expected. That's exactly what I always wanted."

True to the prophecy Augusta described years before, the

Baldwins cofounded Breakthrough Ministry shortly after Stephen began following Jesus. The ministry reaches out to young people involved in extreme sports, such as skateboarding or motocross, with the good news of Jesus. In 2009, Stephen also helped found Now More Than Ever, a ministry designed to reach enlisted men and women with the hope of Jesus.

Those who knew Stephen before Jesus, and even a few who know him now, would have never thought he would be chosen to communicate the words of God. But God has never been in the habit of doing the expected thing. He hasn't done the expected thing in Stephen's life. And he'll surprise you with your life, too, if you let him.

God is speaking. You just have to know where to find his voice. Maybe you've heard his voice in the stories you've read so far in this book. If you have, I hope you will decide to join the chorus of people who have proclaimed, "I Am Second." Giving up your life like that may sound scary. But there is no safer or more satisfying place to be than in the hands of God.

As Stephen described, it means letting the Spirit of God blow your life to whatever corner of the world and on whatever wild ride he has planned—and it truly will be a wild ride!

Ryan Ries can attest to how wild an adventure Jesus really can be. Ryan thought he knew what it meant to live free—then he met the real Jesus.

Chapter 13

Whosoever

the real party

RYAN RIES, RADIO HOST

Ryan Ries knew all about God from his parents. It wasn't more information that he needed, but a personal experience with the divine.

Ryan had grown up hearing the stories from the Bible. His father pastored a large church in Southern California. He traveled the world preaching. Ryan's mother, too, raised her son to follow Jesus.

But Ryan had come to follow someone else.

"I used to have conversations with Satan in my mind," Ryan admits. "If I wanted a girl, I'd ask Satan. I would talk to Satan about success in my life, and he would give me stuff."

Ryan had never planned on following Satan. He hadn't planned for a lot of what happened. He just wanted to party and do his own thing. But what started small eventually grew to monstrous proportions.

"I was always drawn to the other side," he says. "I didn't want what had been force-fed to me at home or in church. I wanted the forbidden fruit."

Ryan followed his own path for a long time. But it wasn't until a difficult breakup that he actually verbalized what he felt toward God.

"I need to tell you something," his girlfriend of a few years told him over the phone. It seemed ominous. She told him she'd had an abortion.

"What?" he said in disbelief.

"I didn't want to involve you."

"We've been dating for all this time. You should be telling me these things."

But just three months later she called again to say she was getting another abortion. Ryan wanted to keep the baby, but she wasn't ready to settle down. She was young and still had other dreams for her life.

"I gave her an ultimatum," Ryan remembers. "If she went through with the abortion, then I would break up with her."

She agreed to a sonogram. The doctor said there were identical twins but one died from vanishing twin syndrome. But they saw the beating heart of the other baby and saw it moving. Ryan was entranced. He could see himself raising a family with this girl. But she couldn't.

They broke up.

"I'm not an emotional guy," he explains. "But that night I was pissed off at God and heartbroken. I was in love. I wanted to start a family with this girl, but now it was over. I was angry with God. I flipped God off, throwing my middle fingers in the air."

At that point Ryan made a deliberate decision to do what he was already doing in practice. He would live the way he wanted to—make money, do drugs, and have all the girls he could.

Fuller realization of what this meant came after a drug-fueled weekend of partying. "I've got pills and a bag of coke," Ryan told his friends. "Come over and we'll party."

The party stretched all through the day. A dozen hits of ecstasy and cocaine burned through Ryan's mind and body. But he'd acclimated to this lifestyle. He could binge one day and go to work the next. It's what came later that really spooked him.

"The next day I came home from work to a terrifying feeling," he recalls. "I lay in bed trying to sleep, and I felt an evil presence in my room. I couldn't explain it."

Admittedly, hallucinogenic drugs have a tendency to give people terrifying visions. "But I was sober at this point," Ryan insists. "I felt something crawl on top of me. It started choking me out."

He tried to scream, but powerful hands gripped his neck and a weight pressed on his chest. His breath lodged in his throat. A black shadow pinned him to the mattress, pressing out his existence. Ryan fought back with desperate fury, but a vise held him fast. Just as blackness crept across his vision, the creature released him. The dark mass of evil popped to one side of the room and then appeared on the other without any movement between. Three times it returned through the night, and three times Ryan clung to life by a thread.

As he lay there in terror, he considered turning to Jesus and asking for deliverance. Ryan had learned about Jesus having power over spirits and demons from his days in church. He could remember sermons and Bible stories that spoke about Jesus casting away such dark presences.

But then he thought of a verse his father had taught him: "You are neither hot nor cold. I wish that you were one or the other! But since you are like lukewarm water, neither hot nor cold, I will spit you out of my mouth!"[1]

Jesus didn't want fake followers. He wanted either hot or cold, in or out, not some kind of in-between, lukewarm pretender. And the truth was, Ryan didn't follow Jesus and wasn't ready to give up his party lifestyle. To call out to Jesus now while following the Devil would make him a hypocrite—"lukewarm," in the words of that verse.

It was one or the other. Ryan knew that. Jesus would require a new way of life. He knew that too. And he wasn't ready for it. So he just lay there all night and hoped the black creature would spare his life.

The next day a friend who had partied with him called. "I saw a black creature with long hair," he told Ryan. "I was sleeping, and it crawled in bed behind me. It put its arms around me."

"Dude, the same thing happened to me!" Ryan responded. "Must have been a hallucination." But he knew better. He knew this was something different—or rather someone different.

This spiritual bondage coupled with a chemical one. Ryan had started smoking cigarettes in junior high. By high school he had graduated to marijuana, cocaine, and eventually a suite of hallucinogenic drugs. All of that had come wrapped up with a crowd of friends and parties until finally his school expelled Ryan and many of his friends. But rather than acting as a wake-up call, his expulsion had only freed him up for more partying.

Eventually Ryan had fallen into the rave scene, which had only fueled his addictions further. Known for the heavy use of electronic music blasted through oversized amplification systems, raves grew out of the rebellious movements of the 1980s and 1990s.

"My brothers were part of the skinhead and punk movements when that whole scene was birthed in LA, and I was influenced by their world-versus-church thinking. I wanted something that went against what my parents were giving me."

The rave parties were set up in secret and unlicensed areas, such as abandoned homes or warehouses. Hidden from authorities, they could rage all through the days and nights and were hotspots of psychoactive drug activities. "You could pop ecstasy pills, use LSD, and hang out in a warehouse with fifty thousand watts of sound for eight hours," he recalls.

Drugs and parties weren't Ryan's only vices. What Ryan would later describe as a sex addiction had first taken root many years before, when he found a duffel bag of pornographic magazines behind his elementary school. He had been six years old at the time. "I didn't know what was going on in those pictures," he says. "But they did something inside my mind and my heart." The images he saw as a child stuck in his head, eventually leading him into a full-blown sex addiction.

"I would use girls like pieces of meat," he admits. "I would party with them for the night, sleep with them, and then peace them out. That was the story."

Ryan soon discovered himself immersed in a world of drugs, promiscuity, and parties. "Everything got deeper," he says. "My life started getting very dark. I ended up overdosing three times. A number of my friends overdosed. I was losing friends who were dying. I was going down, down, down."

At the professional level, however, everything looked good in Ryan's life. He had built a successful career managing professional skateboard teams. He toured the world with these teams, making a lot of money.

"I looked like I had my life together," he remembers. "I had the house. I had the Harleys. I skated the world for a living. But on the inside I was a dead man walking. I kept living this life, taking everything in. But I felt empty, empty, empty. I wasn't content with my life. I was only happy when I was wasted."

The trouble was, after a lifetime of drug use, Ryan actually had difficulty getting wasted. He'd built up tolerance to many substances, making it harder to dull the inner pain. The answer was more and more dangerous cocktails of drugs. "At this point I'm on mushrooms, ecstasy, smoking hash, and drinking. I remember one time when I felt like I was overdosing. I ran to my hotel room, thinking I was dying. I couldn't walk. But after waiting it out, I went outside and bought crack off some guy and started smoking it with him. I woke up the next day and realized I was spinning out of control."

But Ryan couldn't get out of the life he had made for himself. He could see his life slipping away, but he felt powerless to stop it.

At the height of his addiction he would mix ecstasy, heroin, and coke in syringes, while smoking crack. He desperately needed more and more to quiet the unrest in his soul.

Finally, while on a tour through South and Central America with his skateboard team, Ryan hit bottom. A teammate found him unresponsive in bed with cocaine splattered across his face. "They thought I was dead," he says.

"I realized then I had to change my life. I was going to die. It was just a matter of time before I didn't wake up. I was going to die in a hotel room somewhere from an overdose."

So after a nearly two-months-long drug binge, Ryan sobered up and went to his hotel room alone. And that's when he found himself praying to God, "Prove to me that you exist."

He wasn't even sure it was a prayer. Prayer assumes there is a God who is listening. This could just be talking to the ceiling. But if God *was* there, Ryan needed proof—and proof that God cared about Ryan's life. Could God be real, personal, and near?

He recited a prayer his father had taught him years before: "Jesus, forgive me for my sins. Come into my life and fill me with your Holy Spirit." He begged for forgiveness and longed for evidence that it was possible. But still he waffled on the edge of belief and doubt.

"So I challenged God," he says. "I dared him to show me he existed."

Nothing happened.

He opened up the drawer of the nightstand beside him and found a Bible. He took it in his hands and began to read. "I got through a few chapters in the New Testament, then put the Bible down. I was waiting for God to show up. I wanted some kind of supernatural experience."

A lifetime of psychedelic experiences had made him hungry for angels to pop out of the sky. But nothing happened.

Ryan took the Bible for his flight back home. Even though he was holding out for that supernatural experience—some kind of sign or wonder or miracle—he thought that reading a verse or two might help. But once he had picked up the Bible, he couldn't set it down.

"The whole skate team was next to me on the plane," he says. "I knew what they were thinking. *This guy is a pirate! He rents out strip clubs, always has a bag of cocaine, sleeps with all kinds of girls. Now this guy has a Bible?*"

But he felt inexplicably drawn to the book, so once the plane was in the air, he began to read. No signs fell from heaven, and no visits came from the Almighty. But by the time he landed that day, a miracle had indeed occurred.

"I felt peace!" he remembers. "I read for six hours straight on the flight. Then I landed, and I had peace for the first time in my life."

Ryan had spent enormous sums to smoke, inject, and swallow every kind of vision-inducing drug, but this new vision had come through a book. A vision for a new kind of life, a life of peace, became clear in his mind. He had asked for a miracle, thinking that God would visit him as the demon had in his bed years before. He'd read the stories of angels descending, the lame walking, and dead men being raised to life.

But the miracle God gave him was one that catered specially to a restless and tormented soul. It was the miracle of peace.

"This is crazy!" he muttered to himself as he got off the plane.

He woke up the next day to singing in his head—not the loud thump of the raves, but a still, small, musical voice:

> *This is the day the LORD has made.*
> *We will rejoice and be glad in it.*[2]

He recognized the words as something he'd once heard in a Sunday school class. It was a song from the Bible praising God's faithfulness and love. As he sat there listening, more familiar words started flowing through his mind:

> *In my distress I prayed to the LORD,*
> *And the LORD answered me and set me free.*
> *The LORD is for me, so I will have no fear.*[3]

"It kept repeating that over and over and over," he remembers. "I was tripping out at this point. So I decided to call my dad. He could tell me what all this meant."

Ryan told his father all that had been going on with the drugs, the parties, and then the plane ride home. And then, finally, he told his dad that he'd given his life to the Lord.

"The problem," he continued, "is that I keep hearing this song in my head. I think it's from the Bible."

"God is calling you," Ryan's father explained. "That's the Holy Spirit. He has a plan for your life."

With those words, all remaining doubt left Ryan's mind. God had spoken. Ryan had heard him, audibly and real.

He hung up the phone and drove to a store to buy a Bible of his own. At the store he saw a book titled *Save Me from Myself* by recently converted Brian "Head" Welch.[4] He bought both a Bible and the book and immediately began reading.

As he began researching rehabilitation centers where he could get treatment for his drug addiction, he realized another miracle had occurred: he hadn't even thought about drugs for three days. "It's like God just reached down from heaven and yanked the desire out of my life," he remembers. "Any chains that Satan had hooked into me, Jesus ripped them off. He yanked me out of Satan's control completely. I was free."

For most of his life, Ryan Ries had sought freedom. When he was young, it was freedom to think on his own, make his own rules, and follow his own desires. But the life that followed stripped away all the freedom he thought he had. Addictions of all sorts had choked him like the demon in his bed. But now, through Jesus, he was experiencing true freedom.

While still in his party days, Ryan had made friends with Sonny Sandoval, the lead singer of hit rock band P.O.D. He knew that Sonny was now a believer. So he called Sonny, shared his story, and invited him on a trip to Israel.

While in the land of Jesus, Sonny shared an idea with Ryan for a new way of spreading the good news. "I have this name: the Whosoevers," Sonny said. "I see it as a worldwide movement of anyone who loves Jesus to come together and reach the world for Christ."

Ryan liked that idea. Instead of organizing drug-fueled bingers, as he had in his previous life, he would help Sonny organize this new kind of gathering.

He thought back to the Garden of Gethsemane, which they had visited in Israel. Jesus had once prayed in the very same garden, and there he had surrendered everything—his very life—for his Father's mission.

"Not as I will, but as you will," Jesus had prayed.[5] He'd pleaded with the Father for any other way to heal the brokenness in the world. But when the Father told him no, he'd accepted that decision. Jesus would be arrested that very evening, beaten, tortured, and then hung on a cross to die a gruesome and painful death. But even knowing what lay ahead, he offered his obedience and his life for the Father's plan.

Thinking of Jesus' prayer in Gethsemane, Ryan now offered his own prayer of sacrifice. "Do whatever you want in my life," he prayed. "I surrender. It's not my will; it's your will be done from this point forward. I don't even know how I can serve you, but if you want to use me, then show me. Have someone contact me from outside of my immediate circle to have me share my story. I will follow you wherever that takes me. If you call me out, then I'll go."

God called the next day through a pastor in Las Vegas.

"I heard you got saved," the pastor said. "I would love for you to come out and share your story at my church."

Having never shared his story in front of a crowd, Ryan looked for reinforcements. He asked Sonny to go with him. Sonny, in turn, invited his friend Brian "Head" Welch, at that time former guitarist of Korn. Ryan also invited another friend of his, Lacey Sturm of the hit band Flyleaf. They all four walked onto the stage to birth a new movement: The Whosoevers.

Ryan, Sonny, Brian, Lacey, and many others—including,

more recently, Austin Carlile from rock band Of Mice and Men—have joined the movement. They share their stories at rehabilitation centers, schools, concerts, and anywhere else they get a chance. *Live with Ryan Ries* broadcasts on the radio and streams online every Saturday night as part of the same movement, sharing the good news of Jesus.

Ryan grew up a rebel. He sought his own path and made his own rules. But the freedom he sought in the parties, drugs, and girls brought only bondage. Only when he bowed his heart to God, declaring himself second and God first, did he find the greatest high and the truest freedom.

Long ago Jesus warned that "the thief comes only to steal and kill and destroy."[6] The world offers many temptations and countless distractions—drugs, money, sex, and comfort in a thousand forms—but the thief, Satan, hides behind every offering. As Ryan will tell you, there is no freedom or lasting pleasure in any of it. In the end, each leads to destruction and despair.

But Jesus also said, "I have come that [you] may have life, and have it to the full."[7]

Following Jesus means joining a rebellion of epic proportions. It means overwhelming hate with love, overcoming cruelty with kindness, and overthrowing power with meekness. The message of Jesus subverts every establishment of evil, every dominion of oppression.

If you are looking for a purpose, in Jesus you have one. He has a plan for your life, and it's a grand and wonderful plan.

It's something neo-Nazi Michael Kent had a hard time believing could possibly apply to him. But his African American probation officer Tiffany Whittier insisted on sharing with him.

Chapter 14

Hater

love wins

MICHAEL KENT, FORMER NEO-NAZI
TIFFANY WHITTIER, PROBATION OFFICER

"If you love those who love you," Jesus once proposed, "what reward will you get? . . . If you greet only your own people, what more are you doing than others? Even people who are ungodly do that."[1]

Jesus' point was simple. You want to be a good person? Then you'll have to go beyond what everyone else does. All people, no matter how evil, will have someone they love and care for. Even terrorists love their friends and family. If you, too, only love those who love you back, then you are not a good person; you are simply like everyone else.

Jesus taught his people to go beyond average expectations. He demanded a love with no bounds. "Love your enemies," he said. "Pray for those who hurt you. . . . Your Father who is in heaven . . . causes his sun to shine on evil people and good people. He sends rain on those who do right and those who don't. . . . Be perfect, just as your Father in heaven is perfect."[2]

Perfection in the eyes of God is love unbounded and for all: friends, family, neighbors, and, yes, even enemies. When African American probation officer Tiffany Whittier was assigned to white supremacist Michael Kent as her next case, that's exactly what she decided to do.

As a proud holder of white-supremacist ideology, the belief that White people are better than people of other races and should be dominant over them, Michael Kent represented a rising tide in race-related tension. According to the Southern Poverty Law Center, which tracks hate groups and domestic terrorism nationally, the year 2018 capped a four-year rise in race-related hate group membership. Between 2017 and 2018, "extremist-related murders" with race as a motivator spiked 35 percent. Though our justice system has been slow to use the word *terrorism* to describe these race-based hate crimes, which composed the majority of such crimes reported in 2017, they do indeed represent a kind of domestic terrorism.[3] And their repercussions, both physical and emotional, can be devastating.

Looking back at his earlier life with tears in his eyes, Michael Kent now admits the pain that his racist views and actions caused. "I hurt a lot of people," he confesses. "I hurt people when I was a kid. I hurt people when I was an adult."

Although he was never convicted of a hate crime, it was

while in prison for drug- and weapons-related charges that he came to believe in neo-Nazism.[4] With representative groups in countries around the world, neo-Nazism is a particular form of white supremacy that seeks to revive the kind of government-sanctioned hate that brought about the extinction of six million Jewish lives, though paradoxically many in this modern rendition of Hitler's ideology deny that the Holocaust ever happened. Neo-Nazis often get tattoos signifying their allegiances and work to promote their version of hate through rallies, literature, and—these days—especially the internet.

Michael would later grow to even actively promote and grow the movement. "I started getting involved with the higher-ups in the organization," he says. "I helped organize rallies, handing out pamphlets, and going to the state capitol to promote that stuff."

His hate began in part as a response to race-related encounters in his childhood neighborhood. He was bullied by Black children, and his mother was assaulted by a Black man.[5] The trauma of these incidents began to instill a fear and suspicion of African Americans. And then another incident cemented the faulty assumptions he had begun to draw.

"I was twelve years old," Michael remembers. "I had a Black friend. We were thick as thieves. We got along great. One day he invited me over to his house. But then his mom kicked me out."

"I don't want that blue-eyed devil in my house," she demanded.

Michael was never allowed to see or speak to his friend again.

"From that day forward," he determined, "if you don't like me, won't accept me, then it's over."

Hate comes in many forms. People of all colors, shades, and backgrounds find ways to hate on people who look different from them. And when Michael had his first taste of such color-based prejudice, he made a vow to return hate for hate.

Meanwhile, African American probation officer, Tiffany Whittier, grew up and lived with the systemic version of color-based prejudice. Systemic racism in America means that the darker your skin, the steeper the hill that you face, even without everyone involved making knowingly prejudiced discriminations. Black unemployment rates are consistently twice that of Whites. These rates hold true even when accounting for differences in education and work experience.[6] One study even tested this sad reality by sending out resumes identical in every way except one: the name. They found that Emily and Greg were twice as likely to land an interview as Lakisha and Jamal.[7] Hispanics face similar struggles, with the darkness of their skin making a significant difference. Latinos with lighter skin reported rates of discrimination similar to non-Hispanic Whites, whereas darker-skinned Latinos reported a heightened incident of racism.[8]

But despite being surrounded by such an environment, Tiffany made a choice for love, not hate. This held true even when assigned to Michael's case.

"I had an idea of who he was by looking at him on paper," Tiffany says. "I saw the tattoos and his file, but I didn't feel in my gut that I was in danger meeting with him."

Aware that she was about to meet with a dedicated racist, Tiffany drove to Michael's home. It was nighttime. She pulled up in her squad car to a darkened home with a gate in the front.

In her years on the force, Tiffany has learned to listen to her instincts. If something doesn't feel right, it probably isn't. That evening she assessed her surroundings and felt in the clear to walk up to Michael's door and knock. When he answered, he was surprised to see her.

"Are you alone?" Michael asked.

The hairs on the back of Tiffany's neck lifted at the question. The instincts that had given her the clear moments before now shouted danger. Here was a violent white supremacist with an arrest record asking a Black woman, alone and in the dark, if she had anyone with her. She put her hand on her gun in response to his query.

"Yeah," she answered hesitantly. "I'm by myself. Is there a problem?"

But it wasn't violence that came to Michael's mind but respect. He was a person to fear. Even among his friends and neighbors, he instilled a sense of danger. No one came to his house alone, especially at night.

"I gained a lot of respect for her," he says of the visit. "I have never had anyone, even of my own race, come to my house by themselves. She showed up that day, and my eyes were opened to her courage."

Tiffany hadn't thought of herself as brave. She was just doing her job, meeting with her client. But now, after his question, she was feeling foolish.

"They always come in twos," he finally blurted out. "I have respect for you to come to my house by yourself."

If first impressions matter, this one certainly made a mark

on both of them. Michael was impressed with Tiffany's boldness in showing up to his house alone. But as she entered his house, the dominating impression she gained was of hate. A picture of Adolf Hitler hung on Michael's wall. Symbols of racism, violence, and evil crowded his home. She knew her mission would need to go beyond just managing his court-appointed duties. She would need to remake his vision of the world.

People in Tiffany's line of work play an important role in the criminal-justice system. When someone is arrested, their judge can order probation, either before trial or in lieu of prison time. Probation officers oversee and monitor people released under these circumstances. They help their clients by connecting them with state resources that can help rehabilitate them. They make recommendations for counseling, job training, and more. But they also ensure that the offenders carry out their court-ordered requirements, which could involve anything from community service to recovery programs and more.

"He's always been compliant with me," Tiffany says of her neo-Nazi client. "I've had to talk with him about some issues, but he turned it around. I never once thought about revoking his probation, because he did what I asked him to do. He always worked. He made payments toward his probation fines and fees and did what he needed to do."

But when Tiffany and Michael sat down to interview with I Am Second, Michael couldn't let her stop with that assessment. He'd been arrested before. Tiffany wasn't his first probation officer. And she was different. She did more than just ensure compliance and arrange meetings. She cared.

"Why did you help me to change?" he asked.

"It's my job."

"Your job is to make sure I'm abiding by all the laws and not messing up," he said, reflecting on his previous experiences with probation officers. "You were supposed to keep me from committing crimes. But why did you believe in me? That's not your job."

From the first day she showed up at his house, he'd sensed that Tiffany was different. She mixed courage with love, kindness with straight-talking concern. When she saw the pictures of Hitler on his wall, nothing in his court orders required him to take them down. But she knew his heart needed the pictures to go.

"You came into my house and told me to get rid of things that I believed in," he continued. "Why? Why did you care?"

"I wanted you to be a better person," she said. "That's why I do my job."

"But if you had met me in any other circumstance, I would have spit on you," he said. "I don't understand why you took this time. You encouraged me to change my life when my peers and my own people didn't. Probation officers before never wanted to help me. Why did you?"

"I don't know if I have ever told you this, Michael," she said. "But I love you."

Tiffany wasn't confessing romantic feelings, but a deep concern and care for a fellow human being. And when she said it, Michael cried. He knew she did love him. She had proven her care for him in all their meetings during the past few years. She had guided him out of hate, encouraging him to change the books he read, the pictures he hung, and the friends he chose. She had shown her love many times. But now she had said it.

"Why don't we put up smiley faces?" Tiffany would tell him in her meetings with him. "Let's get down Hitler. Let's get down all these racist things. When you go to bed, you can have happy thoughts. When you wake up, you can see smiley faces and not hate."

Michael still can't quite understand why he obeyed her instructions. It's not that she was the first to tell him he needed to get rid of the hate in his life. But she was the first to do it with love and, therefore, the first he could ever really hear.

"You didn't have to do that," he said to her. "I could have been right back in jail if it wasn't for you. I wouldn't be a good father. I wouldn't be a good husband. I wouldn't be the man I am today if it wasn't for your stubbornness and your willingness to push me. I still don't quite get it, but I'm very thankful that you came to my door that day."

Michael came into the interview with a lot of guilt still on his shoulders for the people he'd hurt and the lives he'd ruined with his hate. How could Tiffany love someone like him?

"That's in the past, Michael," she reminded him. "I'm going to tell you how the Lord feels about you. He saw you as a young boy, and he's seen you grow into a man. He wants you to spread his word of love, acceptance, and forgiveness."

"But how can you respect me and accept me with the things I've done?"

"God," she said simply. "You question how you can be forgiven. God forgives no matter how bad our sins are. I forgive you because of God. He's the reason I care for you and how I ended up in your life. But you have to forgive yourself."

"Two years ago I would have said you're a liar," he said. "But I've seen all you've done. I'm a firm believer in that now."

"You've changed me too," she encouraged. "You've helped me."

Before her involvement with Michael, Tiffany would not have described herself as having much attachment to her faith. But in the process of working with him, she saw God's purpose for her life.

"I don't understand why I have so many clients telling me that I've helped as much as I have," she says. "But my sense of purpose and faith in the Lord has grown tremendously in the last several years. I have this strong belief that the Lord is using me."

Since sitting down to interview for this story, Tiffany and Michael have had numerous opportunities to share their story elsewhere. At Martin Luther King Jr.'s ninetieth birthday celebration, Tiffany and Michael were invited by the social-justice leader's daughter Bernice King to tell of their journey from hate to friendship.

"We've had the opportunity to change the way of thinking for so many people," Michael comments on that event and others. "We've shared our story in Australia, China, Germany, and so many places. But when I went to Atlanta for this event, I cried."

"Honestly, it's been overwhelming," Tiffany says. "I'm just a regular person. Since our story went national, it's amazing the impact we have had on people. What I did for Michael came naturally for me. I treat people with respect. I do that with all my clients. I could have gone out to Michael's house with an attitude. But that doesn't change anything. That doesn't help."

Michael spent twenty years of his life in hate and has determined to spend the next twenty years helping people to love.

"It's so easy to love," he says. "It takes much more energy to hate. Racism is a cancer, and it's spreading throughout this country. It will continue to spread until we can get together as one and cure it. What Tiffany did for me was ahead of her time. She could have gotten in trouble for it."

Tiffany, indeed, was ahead of her time. Much of her advice and directions to Michael stretched beyond the normal bounds of the officer-probationer relationship. She went beyond the court's instructions of purely legal adherence and tackled the root cause of Michael's criminal behavior.

"I could throw everyone in jail," Tiffany says of her clients. "There are times I could have arrested Michael for violating his probation terms. But what's that going to do? Now there is a push in my field to work with people, build rapport, and see what really makes them tick. That's the kind of work I did with Michael."

While Tiffany continues in the same role she has filled for years, being hands-on with numerous clients, she also works to inform and train other corrections departments around the country. "The numbers don't lie," she explains. "If you just throw people in jail, that's not helping the problems."

Tiffany's work with Michael didn't just encourage him to leave behind his hate. It also started him on a path to discover the Author of love. He credits the original interview we filmed as a part of I Am Second as a key step in his journey to God.

"You guys opened my eyes," he says. "I cried like a baby. I was too stubborn to believe that I could be doing God's work.

I'd lost faith for many, many years. But after doing this film, it woke something inside of me. I now believe that God has a plan for me."

"When I came back from the I Am Second filming, I was just glowing," Tiffany agreed. "The whole journey has opened my eyes in terms of spirituality. Everything that we have been doing goes back to God. Michael wasn't really a believer before. With all this happening, it has been really cool to see how faith has come into his life. I feel God has been speaking to me even more, guiding me and opening doors. I am God's advocate in a sense. I have restrictions when I'm at work, but I know God's purpose for me being there."

Love wins. In a world full of hate and violence, that truth can be forgotten. But hate only survives in hiding and in the darkness. Love wins by just showing up and knocking on the door.

Tiffany never thought of herself as a world changer. She was just doing her job. She was just loving her clients and helping them change their lives. But it's love that wins in the end. It's love that conquers evil and love that defeats all.

It's tempting to overcomplicate life. You can make endless to-do lists and strive for any number of awards, achievements, or accomplishments. But love is God's ultimate purpose. Love is why he created the universe. Love is why he created you and me. And it's the entire purpose of our time here on earth. Everything else is just window dressing.

Everything you do or experience is a God-given opportunity to love if you can see it that way. If you are looking to change the world and make an impact, remember that the only thing eternal in this life, the only thing that will ever truly last, is the love we give to others. That's how you'll truly make an impact into eternity.

Rudy Kalis is someone who always wanted to make an impact. But after a string of failures, professionally and personally, he doubted if God really had a place for him in his plan.

Chapter 15
Alien

the journey
to belong

RUDY KALIS, SPORTSCASTER

Jesus once told a story about a man with big plans.[1]

Someone in the crowd had come to him for help regarding a family inheritance issue. The man complained that his brother had failed to abide by the law.

"Tell my brother to divide the family property with me," he pleaded with Jesus.

"Watch out!" Jesus warned. "Life is not made up of how much a person has."

Jesus then told a story about a rich farmer who had a bumper crop. His fields produced so plentifully that he ran out of storage space in his barns. He decided to tear down his barns and build bigger ones.

"I'll . . . have plenty of grain stored away for many years," he thought to himself. "Take life easy. Eat, drink, and have a good time."

"You foolish man!" God said in judgment of his plans. "Tonight I will take your life away from you. Then who will get what you have prepared for yourself?"

Jesus then presented his story's moral. "That is how it will be for whoever stores things away for themselves but is not rich in the sight of God."

The Son of God himself had shown up in his questioner's town. The man had one shot to ask anything, to speak with the Lord of creation about whatever he wanted. And what did he ask?

He asked for money.

This issue had surely consumed the man's attention in the days or even weeks leading up to this interaction. Family fights, legal maneuvering, and endless worrying must have filled this man's mind. His father had died, and his brother had taken everything. All was wrong in his world. But rather than fixing the man's troubles, Jesus sought to fix his focus. The man was clinging to the wrong worries, the wrong life plans, and the wrong riches.

Like everyone else in the world, you, too, probably have dreams and plans for the future. Whether those plans are big or small, whether they are for tomorrow or for twenty years down the road, you have things you want to see happen in your life.

But are they God's plans or yours?

Maybe you long ago gave up on ever seeing your plans come to fruition and have let bitterness and resentment take their place. Or maybe you've thrown so much at those plans that you've given your very soul to achieve them. If this is you, sportscaster Rudy Kalis has a story he wants you to hear.

Rudy had many hopes and dreams for the future. He had his own set of plans. But only when he trusted God for his future did he find the success he longed for.

Rudy was born into an immigrant family of desperate means. His father had served in the Russian army during World War II and been captured by the Germans. The war had killed nearly 3 percent of the world's population, or sixty million people, including fifteen million battle deaths and another forty-five million civilian deaths. His father survived on the bloodiest front, where at least one-third of those deaths occurred.

Finally, in the opening months of 1945, Allied forces marched through Germany, liberating millions of prisoners of war, including Rudy's dad. Rudy was born after his parents met in a refugee camp. But the end of the war didn't end the suffering.

Between 1945 and 1951, Europe hosted upwards of twenty million displaced persons. With many cities devastated and unlivable, lands conquered and reconquered, and shifting country borders, millions had no home to call their own. A host of Central and Eastern Europeans found themselves in foreign lands following the war, when German territory was split among the victors.[2]

It was from this scene of chaos and misery that Rudy and his family came to the shores of America. "We came to the United States on a ship," Rudy says. "I remember coming into New York and seeing the Statue of Liberty. People cried."

The US government issued the family a portion of money

and train tickets west. Five-year-old Rudy and his family stepped off the train in Milwaukee, Wisconsin.

"I didn't know how to speak English," he recalls. "I remember going to school and coming home crying every day. The kids were laughing at me."

In time he and the rest of his family learned English and adjusted to their new context. But Rudy always struggled with the language and culture and never could catch on like his sister. His parents made the comparison clear. "You're never going to amount to anything," he remembers them saying. His sister got straight As. Rudy didn't. He struggled to meet expectations and wondered if perhaps something really was wrong with him.

"I never felt good enough," he remembers. "I grew up never having a real sense of confidence about myself. My parents never knew how to encourage me."

After getting through high school, Rudy attempted college but flunked out after just one year. Everywhere he turned, he found failure and struggle.

"These things sat inside of me," he says. "I never thought I'd be good at anything."

After being drafted into the Vietnam War, he enlisted in the United States Air Force. After completing his service, however, he returned to college and started again with new vigor. He pushed through his classes and found hope for validation in broadcasting. He knew he'd never be a professional athlete himself, but sports broadcasting could at least put him next to the action and in the general sphere of success.

Rudy graduated and found a job as a reporter at a small

television studio in Green Bay, Wisconsin. Less than two years into the job, the sports director quit. This was the opportunity Rudy had longed for.

"I always figured if I was in the right place at the right time, I'd get the job," he says. "I thought this would be it." He spent a month filling in and auditioning for the job, working seven days a week. This was his passion.

"My wife and I were married at a very young age," he says. "We were both looking for the fast lane to success and so working countless hours never phased us."

The studio hired consultants to help find the right replacement. They called Rudy into the office and gave him their assessment of his month of auditioning.

"Rudy, you're a friendly guy," they told him afterward. "But you're never going to make it. You ought to get out of broadcasting."

Not good enough again.

"It was the same thing all over again," he says. "I wasn't good enough at school. Coach would tell me I wasn't good enough at sports. Now I'm not good enough for broadcasting."

He shoved the disappointment aside and pushed even harder.

"You find out your level of determination when something like that happens," he says. "I was determined to prove them wrong." He sent résumés out and finally won another position at a television studio in Nashville, Tennessee.

"I figured I was back on track," Rudy says of his career ambitions at the time.

Meanwhile, Rudy's wife never adapted to living away from her family and friends back in Wisconsin.

"Pride, on both our parts, pulled us further apart," he says. "We got married too young. Though our daughter was born in Nashville, we eventually separated and divorced." Their daughter was three years old at the time and stayed with Rudy in Nashville.

The whole episode left him feeling like a failure. Not good enough in everything he'd done.

Sometime later, a new position opened up at the Nashville station. The sports director left for another opportunity and Rudy applied for the position. He was passed over again.

He would later find himself driving down the interstate pounding the steering wheel of his car.

"God help me!" he cried out. "I'm just sick and tired of being phony."

Rudy hadn't said a prayer since he was nineteen years old and he had headed off to the air force. But he had come to his end. For too long he'd put on the brave face of determination. He would make it in broadcasting one day, he'd told the world. His dream would come true. But inside he knew he was just a failure and a fake. The voices had been right. He'd never amount to anything.

These thoughts welled up in him as he pulled in and found a seat alone at a little restaurant in town.

"Are you all right?" a man asked, pulling up a seat. "It looks like something is bothering you."

"I'm fine," Rudy insisted. "Really, I am."

But the man saw through his denials.

"What's really going on in your life?" he asked.

At that Rudy broke down. He had failed at school. He'd failed at marriage and fatherhood. He'd failed at broadcasting. His dreams and his plans had all come to nothing. Maybe there really was something wrong with him.

"God loves you," the man said. "And he has a plan for your life. You just have to trust him."

Rudy had not heard anything like this since he attended a Christian school as a child and into high school. He hadn't paid attention to these things then—too young and too busy wanting to be somebody with plans for his life. But now, broken, the words came alive in his heart. God loved him? He had a plan for his life? Could it really be true? The man's words drew him in enough that he agreed to meet the man for lunch the following day.

"Would you like to pray and ask Jesus Christ to be the Lord of your life?" the man asked when they met again. Rudy had been the lord of his own life up until then. He'd had his own plan and his own dreams, but none of them had worked out. The harder he'd tried, the worse he'd failed.

With not much else to lose, he decided to give God the reins.

"I didn't walk out of there with a halo around my head," he remembers. "But something inside of me was burning. I needed to know more about this God that I'd just given my life to."

Rudy took up the Bible and began reading. The first thing to change was his perspective.

"I began to look into other people's eyes," he says. "I began to think about something other than myself. Ego had always been my biggest problem. That had been the downfall of everything for me."

Media personalities are bred to think, *Me first.* It's in the DNA of someone who believes so much in their opinions that they paste their own faces on every screen, billboard, and article they can manage.

"I'm in an ego-driven business," Rudy admits. "You have to brag on who you are. You have to strut your stuff everywhere. You have to be first."

But God showed him a different path. Verse after verse stuck out to him as he read the Bible.

> The reward for humility and fear of the LORD
> is riches and honor and life.[3]

> When pride comes, then comes disgrace.[4]

> Seek first his kingdom . . . and all these things will be given
> to you as well.[5]

These verses and others began a transformation in Rudy's heart.

"It even led to me meeting the woman of my dreams," he says of his now wife, Leigh. They recently celebrated their fortieth anniversary together.

"I could be so cynical," Rudy says of himself. "I could be negative and critical, which is so popular in media now. But God showed me that the way I do my work impacted other people. Somehow we think that people who are in your face and know it all are more intelligent. It doesn't work that way. That's not the way God intended it. God showed me to look into other people's eyes and listen to them and realize that I impact thousands by the spirit with which I do my work on television."

Soon Rudy was applying what he was learning to his work in sports broadcasting. In the world of sports, everyone has an opinion and is convinced that opinion is right.

"They ought to fire that coach!"

"Get him off the field!"

"What a dumb play!"

But God began to show Rudy that good listening would get him further than loud opinions.

"The more I've grown in Christ, the more my life is diametrically opposed to what's considered successful in this business. Everything in my work is to be first. Jam it down people's throats. You know all the answers. But God just kept saying to me, 'Be humble. Be a servant.'"

As Rudy began pairing humbleness with confidence, God's plan for his life unfolded. He developed a reputation for his first-person feature stories, which showed him doing everything from skydiving to driving race cars to flying in an F-16 fighter jet. His ability to listen, empathize, and care about the people he interviewed translated into must-watch television that spanned five decades.

In his forty-three years since joining News 4 in Nashville, Rudy has won four regional Emmy Awards, fifteen Associated Press awards for outstanding sportscast in Tennessee, and one National Journalism award for a locally produced documentary. He rose from field reporter to sports director and finally to coanchor before retiring from full-time work at the end of 2017. He's been inducted into three Halls of Fame, including, ironically, his high school in Milwaukee, where he struggled so much.

Through it all, he learned to trust the One who directs his steps.

"When I don't know what to do, I know that God does," he says. "He'll just guide me along. I don't know where it ends. I don't know how far it goes. All I know is that I'm in his hands. He took this dumb little kid from another country who couldn't speak English, stuttered, and made a lot of mistakes and somehow guided him along so that he's able to touch other lives. That's the real joy of my life."

Since retiring, Rudy has found a second calling in life, one that's even bigger than the first. "I have literally realized that I spent all these years in broadcasting and communicating just to prepare me for this greater work," Rudy says of his full-time volunteer work with Men of Valor. This faith-based ministry reaches into prisons to share the good news of Jesus with those in greatest need of this message of hope. He speaks with gang members, men on death row, and others, sharing with them that God has a plan for their lives. Life has certainly come full circle for Rudy, which is why one of his favorite passages in the Bible says, "The heart of man plans his way, but the LORD establishes his steps."[6]

How to Become **Second**

Becoming second means recognizing that God is first. It means believing and trusting in Jesus and accepting who he is and what he did. The stories of I am Second illustrate the peace, purpose, and freedom that many people experienced when they made the decision to be second. But the thread that holds each of these stories together is not so much what they got out of their experiences but where they began.

They each began by understanding they were broken people. They each believed they were sinners. Nobody escapes the weaknesses of being human. No one is without failures and mistakes, pride or selfishness. Everyone fails to love as they should.

These sins or failures separate people from God. They also bring a punishment. According to Romans 6:23, "The wages of sin is death." Because of sin, everyone will face judgment when they die. "People are destined to die once, and after that to face judgment."[1]

God does not judge whether someone did more right than wrong. Perfection is the standard. Sin at any level, any amount, makes one guilty. Even in the present-day world, a person who commits a crime is not judged by whether he has done more good than he has wrong. He is judged by whether or not he committed the crime.

Those who depend on their own good works are destined to spend eternity separated from God in hell. But God offers forgiveness for all these sins. He offers forgiveness through faith in Jesus.

It starts with an admission of guilt, a change of mind, a willingness to start going God's way instead of going our own way. It involves admitting we are full of sin and in desperate need of help. But it is not just any help we must look for, but Jesus' help. It is Jesus we need. It is his message and sacrifice that we must accept and believe to experience forgiveness and a relationship with God. We will be saved from our own desperation by faith in the God of the Bible and in his Son, Jesus.

So who is this Jesus?

Jesus Is First

It's not about us. It's not about our good deeds or religion. It's about who Jesus is and what he did. "For what we preach is not ourselves, but Jesus Christ as Lord, and ourselves as your servants for Jesus' sake."[2] It's about Jesus, always and fully God, who came to earth and was born a baby in full humanity, who later died on a cross for our sins, and who was raised to life on the third day after his death.

Jesus Died to Forgive Our Sins

The message of Jesus is simple and is summarized in 1 Corinthians 15:1–4:

Now, brothers and sisters, I want to remind you of the gospel I preached to you, which you received and on which you have taken your stand. By this gospel you are saved, if you hold firmly to the word I preached to you . . . that Christ died for our sins according to the Scriptures, that he was buried, that he was raised on the third day according to the Scriptures.

Without the death of Jesus, there would be no forgiveness of sins.

Jesus Rose from the Dead

The foundation of our faith is not our personal story. The foundation of our faith is a historic event: the resurrection of Jesus. Paul wrote, "And if Christ has not been raised, your faith is futile; you are still in your sins."[3]

We Are Saved by God's Grace, Not by Good Works

We do not earn forgiveness. It is a gift. "Now to the one who works, wages are not credited as a gift but as an obligation. However, to the one who does not work but trusts God who justifies the ungodly, their faith is credited as righteousness."[4] God expects our behavior and life to change after we trust him, but this change does not save us.

We Are Saved by Grace through Faith

This gift is received through believing. "For it is by grace you have been saved, through faith—and this is not from yourselves, it is the gift of God—not by works, so that no one can boast."[5]

If you want to be second, if you believe in Jesus—who he is and what he did—take a moment right now and tell him. Do you want to be forgiven of your wrongs and weaknesses? Then tell him. God has promised to forgive any and all who ask. Do you want to follow Jesus and receive the new life he offers? Then tell him. God offers forever life to any who ask and believe in Jesus and all he did. Do you want to leave your old, broken life and start anew? Then begin that journey today by telling him, "I am second. You are first."

What Do I Do Now?

Following Jesus is a group activity. No one does it alone. We have a team of coaches in cities across the country and online who can partner with you to develop a plan for your new life. They will help you connect with others in your area who have also become second, talk with God through prayer, understand your faith by learning to study and live out the Bible, and much more.

Visit www.iamsecond.com/live-second to talk with someone today.

Notes

INTRODUCTION

1. Cigna study found here on page 3 of the document: https://www
.ipsos.com/sites/default/files/ct/news/documents/2018-05/us
-loneliness-index-report-pr-2018-05-01.pdf. "Any Anxiety
Disorder," National Institute of Mental Health, https://www
.nimh.nih.gov/health/statistics/any-anxiety-disorder.shtml.

CHAPTER 1: LEGACY

1. Belinda Luscombe, "The Divorce Rate Is Dropping. That May
Not Actually Be Good News," *Time*, November 26, 2018, https://
time.com/5434949/divorce-rate-children-marriage-benefits/.

2. Hal Arkowitz, Scott O. Lilienfeld, "Is Divorce Bad for Children?"
Scientific American, May 1, 2013, https://www.scientificamerican
.com/article/is-divorce-bad-for-children/.

3. "National Statistics on Child Abuse," National and Children's
Alliance, accessed April 15, 2020, https://www
.nationalchildrensalliance.org/media-room/nca-digital
-media-kit/national-statistics-on-child-abuse/.

4. David and Tamela Mann, *Us Against the World* (Nashville:
Thomas Nelson, 2018), 7.

CHAPTER 2: DREAMS

1. Genesis 12:1 NIRV.
2. Genesis 17:5.

CHAPTER 3: STALKER

1. 1 Samuel 17; 2 Samuel 21:22.
2. The story of David's troubles before becoming king can be found in 1 Samuel 16–31.
3. 1 Samuel 13:14 and Acts 13:22.
4. Psalm 13:1.
5. Matthew 11:28.

CHAPTER 4: COMEBACK

1. James 1:2–4 NIRV.
2. Psalm 46:2–3, 10–11 NIRV.

CHAPTER 5: CHOICES

1. James 4:13–15 NIRV.

CHAPTER 6: UNWORTHY

1. For more information about this organization and what it does, visit Rachelschallenge.org.
2. Some of this account, including dialogue, is taken from Mike Sager, Sandra G. Boodman, et al., "21 Hours of Rage, Fear and Suspense at Lake Braddock School," *Washington Post*, November 12, 1982, https://www.washingtonpost.com/archive/local/1982/11/12/21-hours-of-rage-fear-and-suspense-at-lake-braddock-school/21c59ce7-c09a-40a1-b662-333df343a4d7/.
3. Celina Durgin, "Jesus Stopped Me from a Shooting Rampage," *Christianity Today*, October 21, 2019, https://www.christianitytoday.com/ct/2019/october-web-only/jesus-stopped-me-from-shooting-rampage.html.
4. Justin William Moyer, "'I Was Always Hiding My Face': The Bizarre Life of Virginia's Redeemed School Shooter," *Washington*

Post, May 4, 2018, https://www.washingtonpost.com/local/i-was
-always-hiding-my-face-the-bizarre-life-of-virginias-redeemed
-school-shooter/2018/05/03/cdfd2cdc-2ba2-11e8-9dde
-2465d8a02a6c_story.html.

5. Durgin, "Jesus Stopped Me."

6. Luke 23:34.

7. Ephesians 2:8–9.

CHAPTER 7: VALLEYS

1. Mark 8:34 NLT.

2. Verses 35–37 NLT.

3. Genesis 32:22–32.

4. Jeremiah 29:11, 13–14.

CHAPTER 8: AFTERMATH

1. Ezekiel 36:26.

2. For more information about the Mighty Oaks Foundation and its
Warrior Programs, visit https://www.mightyoaksprograms.org/.

CHAPTER 9: ADOPTED

1. Child Welfare Information Gateway, *Planning for Adoption:
Knowing the Costs and Resources*, fact sheet provided by US
Department of Health and Human Services, Children's Bureau,
November 2016, https://www.childwelfare.gov/pubpdfs/s_costs.pdf.

2. Child Welfare Information Gateway, *Foster Care Statistics 2017*,
fact sheet provided by US Department of Health and Human
Services, Children's Bureau, March 2019, https://www
.childwelfare.gov/pubPDFs/foster.pdf.

3. Zechariah 7:9–10 NIRV.

4. Psalm 146:9.

5. Cathy Payne, "Adoption Numbers Rising for Kids in Foster
Care," *USA Today*, August 12, 2013, https://www.usatoday.com
/story/news/nation/2013/08/12/adoption-foster-care/2643505/.

CHAPTER 10: WHOLE

1. Ephesians 1:4–5 NIRV.
2. "The Siberian Parents Who Gave Up Jessica Long As a New-Born Baby Salute Her Heroic Achievement," *Siberian Times*, September 15, 2012, https://siberiantimes.com/sport/profile /features/the-siberian-parents-who-gave-up-jessica-long-as-a -new-born-baby-salute-her-heroic-achievement/.
3. This story is found in Luke 15:11–32.

CHAPTER 11: REBORN

1. Andrew Gelman, Jeffrey Fagan, and Alex Kiss, "An Analysis of the New York City Police Department's 'Stop-and-Frisk' Policy in the Context of Claims of Racial Bias," *Journal of the American Statistical Association* 102, no. 479 (September 2007): 822, https:// doi.org/10.1198/016214506000001040.
2. James 2:5.
3. Matthew 5:14, 16.

CHAPTER 12: MAID

1. His story can be found in Numbers 22. It is paraphrased here, with some of the dialogue coming from the NIRV.
2. Stephen Baldwin with Mark Tabb, *The Unusual Suspect: My Calling to the New Hardcore Movement of Faith* (New York: FaithWords, 2006), 12.
3. This story is found in John 3:1–12. It is paraphrased here, but dialogue is taken from the NIRV.

CHAPTER 13: WHOSOEVER

1. Revelation 3:15–16 NLT.
2. Psalm 118:24 NLT.
3. Psalm 118:5–6 NLT.
4. Brian "Head" Welch, *Save Me from Myself: How I Found God,*

Quit Korn, Kicked Drugs, and Lived to Tell My Story (New York: HarperCollins, 2009).

5. Matthew 26:39 ESV.

6. John 10:10.

7. John 10:10.

CHAPTER 14: HATER

1. Matthew 5:46–47 NIRV.

2. Matthew 5:44–45, 48 NIRV.

3. Elisha Fieldstadt and Ken Dilanian, "White Nationalism-Fueled Violence Is on the Rise, but FBI Is Slow to Call It Domestic Terrorism," NBC News (website), August 5, 2019, https://www .nbcnews.com/news/us-news/white-nationalism-fueled-violence -rise-fbi-slow-call-it-domestic-n1039206.

4. Lindsey Bever, "The 'Ironic' Friendship That Convinced a Former Neo-Nazi to Erase His Swastika Tattoos," *Washington Post*, October 7, 2017, https://www.washingtonpost.com/news /inspired-life/wp/2017/10/07/the-ironic-friendship-that -convinced-a-former-neo-nazi-to-erase-his-swastika-tattoos/.

5. Bever, "The 'Ironic' Friendship," *Washington Post*.

6. Drew Desilver, "Black Unemployment Rate Is Consistently Twice That of Whites," Pew Research Center, FactTank, August 21, 2013, https://www.pewresearch.org/fact-tank/2013/08/21 /through-good-times-and-bad-black-unemployment-is -consistently-double-that-of-whites/.

7. Marianne Bertrand and Sendhil Mullainathan, "Are Emily and Greg More Employable than Lakisha and Jamal?: A Field Experiment on Labor Market Discrimination," NBER Working Paper 9873, National Bureau of Economic Research (website), July 2003, https://www.nber.org/papers/w9873.

8. Ana Gonzalez-Barrera, "Hispanics with Darker Skin Are More Likely to Experience Discrimination than Those with Lighter

Skin," Pew Research Center FactTank, July 2, 2019, https://www
.pewresearch.org/fact-tank/2019/07/02/hispanics-with-darker
-skin-are-more-likely-to-experience-discrimination-than
-those-with-lighter-skin/.

CHAPTER 15: ALIEN

1. Story retold from Luke 12:13–15. Story is paraphrased but dialogue is taken from the NIRV version.
2. Mark Wyman, *DPs: Europe's Displaced Persons, 1945–1951* (Ithaca, NY: Cornell University Press, 1998).
3. Proverbs 22:4 ESV.
4. Proverbs 11:2.
5. Matthew 6:33.
6. Proverbs 16:9 ESV.

HOW TO BECOME SECOND

1. Hebrews 9:27.
2. 2 Corinthians 4:5.
3. 1 Corinthians 15:17.
4. Romans 4:4–5.
5. Ephesians 2:8–9.

About the Author

Doug Bender is a writer and a small-groups coach for the I Am Second movement and organization. He developed many of the tools found at iamsecond.com and has coached churches, organizations, and individuals to use I Am Second groups to share the message of Jesus with their friends and family. He works with I Am Second's parent organization, e3 Partners Ministry, as a church planter and pastor in countries such as Ethiopia, Colombia, and the United States. He also pastors a church just outside of Pittsburgh, Pennsylvania. Doug and his wife, Catherine, have four children: Bethany, Samuel, Isabella, and Jesse.

I Am Second:
Real Stories. Changing Lives

Read the original national bestseller.

Countless stories. One incredible ending.

A major league baseball player. A Tennessee pastor. A reality TV star. A single mom. A multi-platinum rocker. What do these people have in common? They've all hit bottom. And none of them stayed there.

Shocking in their honesty, inspiring in their courage, these stories are critical reminders that no one is too far from God to find him. Join these and thousands more who have discovered the life-changing power in putting God first and proclaiming, "I Am Second."

Live Second:
365 Ways to Make Jesus First

If these incredible stories of changed lives have inspired or challenged you to reevaluate your relationship with God, then pick up this daily reader with 365 readings, prayers, action steps, and an online community of support designed as a tool for you to Live Second.

I Choose Peace:

Raw stories of real people finding contentment and happiness by Doug Bender

Peace. We are all looking for it. We all need it. Yet for many, it remains just out of reach. But peace can be found. *I Choose Peace* tells the stories of people who searched everywhere for fulfillment and wholeness but found it only when they put Jesus first in their lives. Raw, compelling, and profoundly inspiring, the stories in *I Choose Peace* remind us that no matter your struggle, what you've done, or what's been done to you, you can still choose peace.

Watch the Films

Watch the raw, inspiring, real stories of real people learning to live for something greater than themselves at **iamsecond.com.**

Follow and Connect

Get daily updates, inspiration, stories, and more when you follow I Am Second on Instagram, Facebook, Twitter, or YouTube.

Join the I Am Second Community

Get free exclusive access to all 140+ I Am Second films, behind-the-scenes content, practical tools for your spiritual journey, and a community of people living Second.

Wear, Live, Share the Message

Wear the gear that is sure to start a conversation. Get apparel, wristbands, and more. Everything you need to make a statement is at **iamsecondstore.com.**

I AM SECOND